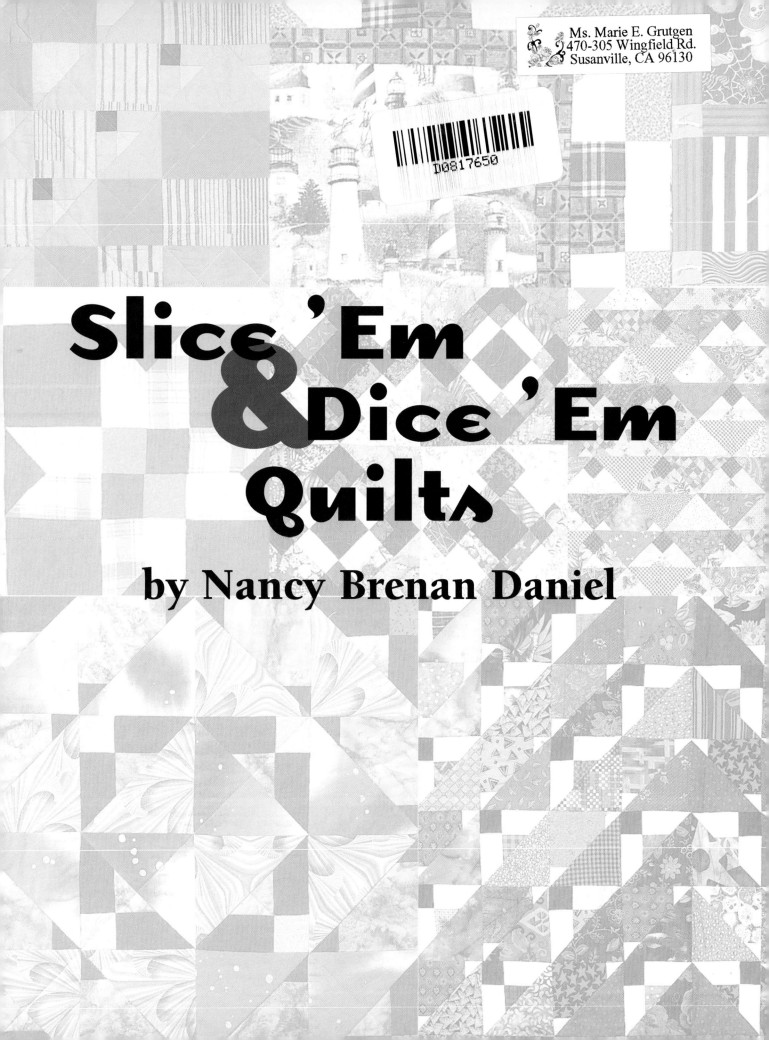

Slice 'Em & Dice 'Em Quilts

by Nancy Brenan Daniel

Linda Causee, Editor

Carol Wilson Mansfield, Photo Stylist

Wayne Norton, Photography

Graphic Solutions inc-chgo, Book Design

Produced by The Creative Partners™

Introduction

As a traveling teacher, it's fairly common to be asked to give a very short demonstration of a fun trick or tip we have developed. It was just such a request that sent me scurrying to my stash of very old Nine-Patch blocks and an almost forgotten idea I had earlier… "How to turn some pretty ugly Nine-Patch blocks into something… well, less ugly."

I had made the Nine-Patch blocks over time while teaching "newbe" quilters to track a one-quarter inch seam allowance. While I had made the blocks as only instructional tools, I'm frugal enough that I don't throw any block that I've sewn away. After all, I had invested time and ugly fabric in those things. These Nine-Patch blocks were made from the dregs of my stash.

Some of the experimental Nine-Patch blocks had fabric added to them. Some had been sliced and diced until one hardly recognized their original design—the Nine Patch. Dozens, if not hundreds, of these blocks had been used in various other projects, but there was a handful of them left – like bread-crumbs – enough to lead me back to that almost forgotten idea.

My Slice 'em & Dice 'em Disappearring Nine-Patch demonstration was a huge hit at the quilt show in Paducah, Kentucky. The women who watched that first demonstration were intrigued by what they witnessed and almost without exception said, "…I'll never remember that…you need to teach a class."

When I returned from Paducah, I carefully put away my teaching samples – including the ones for the Nine-Patch ideas – and didn't look at them again for about four years. That was when Judy Murrah of Quilts Inc. asked me to teach a half-day rotary technique class during the International Quilt Festival in Houston, Texas.

The rest is history. I've now taught thousands of quilters to slice and dice Nine-Patch blocks to create new and interesting quilts and to incorporate the design techniques into their work in meaningful ways.

Many other quilts and ideas emerge while I play with Nine Patches. This book will introduce you to twenty of the newest of the vanishing Nine-Patch quilts.

Have fun.

Nancy Brenan Daniel

Contents

Easy Does It

Trip Around the Scrap Basket

Arizona Road Trip

Spring Baskets

Watermelon Baskets

Blue OP

Floating Grid

Large Blue Star

Tuscan Stars

Jelly Beans
26

Scrap Bag Shadow Boxes
31

The Village
39

Lattice
43

Autumn Stars
70

Small Medallion
75

Blue Medallion
80

Dragonfly
84

Nautical Stars
113

Plaid Stars
117

Provincial Stars
124

General Directions

PLANNING YOUR QUILT SIZE

Many quilts you make can be any size you desire. Sometimes a lap quilt could fit a crib or it might be closer in size to a twin bed cover. A wall quilt, for example, can mean almost any size one could imagine.

FITTING A BED

There are many ways to fit a quilt to a bed. It will depend on the style of quilt and its intended use on the bed. My Grandma Ritzenthaler, for example, made her quilts to fit the top of a mattress under a bedspread. The only exception I know of was the quilt she made for the twin bed in my dormitory room at the university. This quilt, in red and white, was custom-fitted to the bed and was used both as a bedspread and for additional warmth against the cold winters in Bloomington, Indiana.

TYPES OF BEDCOVERS

Spread/Blanket

A spread/blanket does not include a pillow tuck. It can hang to the depth of the first mattress and be tucked under. It can also be a few inches larger than the mattress and used as a blanket. It is the most casual bedcover used for bunk and platform mattress covers as well as for extra warmth.

Comforter/Duvet

This style of bedding does not include a pillow tuck and drops only to the depth of the mattress on three sides. The comforter lies flat. Decorative pillows and pillows in shams are at the head of the bed.

Bedspread

A bedspread drops almost to the floor on three sides or a few inches past the top mattress when there is a dust ruffle. It includes a pillow tuck.

Custom Quilts

Referring to **Diagrams 1**, **2** and **3**, measure the dimensions of the mattress while it is fitted with a mattress pad, sheets and blankets. Include the depth of your mattress in your calculations. Many contemporary mattresses have extra pillow tops that will add considerably to the depth of the mattress creating the need for wider and longer quilts. Other size considerations: the height of the bed; whether or not it has a box spring; whether or not a dust ruffle is being used on the bed; and whether or not a pillow tuck is included. A pillow tuck will add eight to twelve inches to the length of the quilt. By deciding how you will use your quilt, you can plan and design it to fit properly.

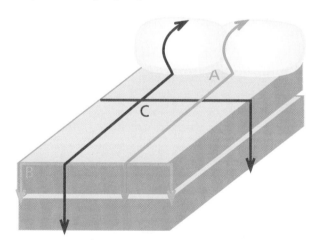

A - Bedspread with pillow tuck
B - Bedspread with dust ruffle
C - Bedspread to the floor

Diagram 1

6

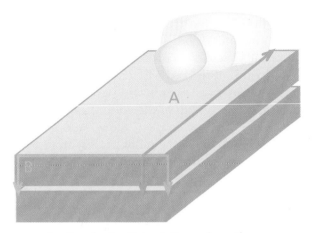

A - Comforter/Duvet Cover length
B - Comforter/Duvet Cover width

Diagram 2

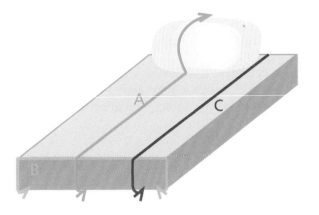

A - Spread with pillow tuck
B - Spread with tuck under
C - Spread with no pillow tuck

Diagram 3

Tip: *Use a flexible tape measure to provide the most accurate measurements.*

The following is a listing of standard, traditional mattress sizes. Use it only as a guide. It does not represent the myriad of mattress and bedding sizes available today. Fill in the blanks with the measurements for your ideal quilt.

Hint: *Quilting causes shrinkage in the finished size of the quilt top. It's better to plan a slightly larger quilt. The more heavily the quilting, the more shrinkage will occur.*

Description	Mattress	Spread/Blanket	Comforter/Duvet	Bedspread
Large Crib	27" x 52"	_____	_____	_____
Playpen	40" x 40"	_____	_____	_____
Bunk	38" x 75"	_____	_____	_____
Twin	39" x 75"	_____	_____	_____
Double	54" x 75"	_____	_____	_____
Queen	60" x 80"	_____	_____	_____
King	76" x 80"	_____	_____	_____
Cal. King	72" x 84"	_____	_____	_____

Adapting Quilt Designs

There are several ways to adapt the quilts in this book to accommodate your needs. To change a quilt size, one can plan to add or delete rows of blocks and increase or decrease the number or size of the borders. Every change in size will affect the yardage required. Several of the quilts include size variations along with the yardage required.

Retrofitting Quilts

We most often think of bedcovers and quilts, in particular, as being squares or rectangles. You may need to modify the shape of a quilt under special circumstances. For example, if your quilt is for a post bed, you may want to consider cutting away the corners at the foot of the bed. Where these corner cuts are made will depend on how your bed is constructed. You can plan for the corner cuts while you design the quilt or you can simply cut the corners after the quilting but before attaching the binding. **(Diagram 4)**

Diagram 4

If your quilt is a comforter size, without a pillow tuck, and you later decide you want a pillow cover, you can make a separate cover to fit over the pillows. The width of the bed will determine the width of the pillow cover. The depth and size of the pillow will determine the length of the cover. Add about 16" to the length of the cover to allow for tucking under the pillows. Make the pillow covers from the same fabrics as the quilt coordinating the quilt design into the cover design. **(Diagram 5)**

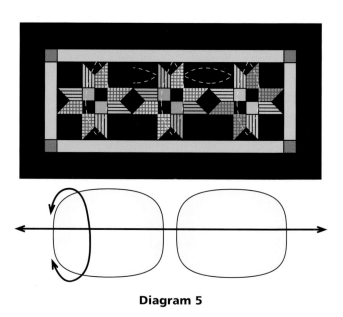

Diagram 5

FABRIC SELECTION AND PREPARATION

Selecting fabrics for your rapidly-cut and pieced quilts may be the most important part of the planning. Fabric yardage for all quilts is estimated for 42"-44" wide fabrics.

Plan for and buy 3/4 yard more fabric when using a highly-directional print. This allows a 27" cut on the lengthwise, straight grain.

Select fabrics that do not stretch excessively while being cut and do not fray at the cut edge. Choose 100% cottons for their ease and consistency in handling. Cotton fabrics hold their shape and are easy to cut and sew accurately. Cotton blends may be combined with 100% cotton fabrics if they are of equal weight, thickness, weave and stability. If you choose to use 100% cotton fabrics and blends together in the same project, be aware it will require extra care in cutting, sewing and pressing.

Pre-wash all fabrics. All woven fabrics will have some residual shrinkage. The tightness of the weave and the quality represented by the maker's name can have some relevance to the amount of shrinkage one can expect. Wash and rinse all fabric until the water runs clear of excess dyes.

Iron the fabric to remove wrinkles. If washing removes too much body from the fabric, use spray sizing or starch when ironing. Returning this extra body to the fabric also makes it easier to cut either by scissors or rotary cutter.

Take extra care when ironing blended cotton/polyester or other blends. Most blends are very sensitive to the hot temperatures used to iron 100% cotton fabrics.

Grain Lines

Note: Refer to **Diagram 6** *for the following information on grain line.*

Selvage

The selvages of yardage are the parallel edges of the warp of the woven material. Lengthwise cuts made parallel to a selvage edge are the most stable. Always trim selvage from yardage before use.

Crosswise Grain

The woven threads of yardage, the weft, have more give than the warp. Strips cut on the crosswise grain show little difference in direction of the cut.

Bias

True bias is a 45-degree angle to the selvage—a diagonal line, 45 degrees between the lengthwise and the crosswise grain. A bias cut edge of fabric has the most stretch and must be handled carefully when sewing and pressing.

STRAIGHTENING YOUR FABRIC

Fabric is rarely cut on the grain when purchased. First, straighten it by pulling gently along the bias in one direction and then pull in other direction. **(Diagram 7)** Fabric is easier to pull straight after it has been washed.

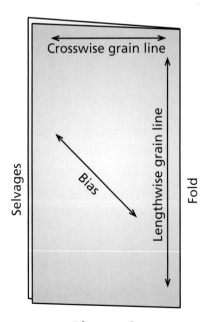

Diagram 6

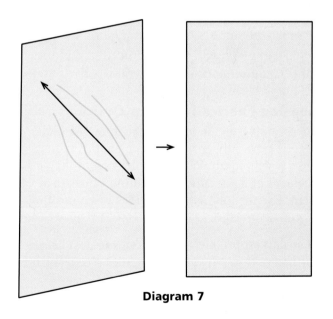

Diagram 7

9

FABRICS FOR SCRAP TECHNIQUES

Whether you buy, reclaim, or trade your small pieces of 100% cotton fabrics, you can put them all into a modern-day scrap quilt. Scrap quilts made from remnants leftover from clothing or decorating construction is our oldest quilt making tradition. Today, the reality is that most of us construct our scrap quilts from the remains of other quilt or decorating projects, fat quarters or even smaller fabric cuts from the quilt shop.

Some quilting guilds and organizations identify a scrap quilt as having more than fifty fabrics—other groups require other amounts or percentages. Don't worry about the labels or artificial distinctions. If you think it is a scrap quilt…call it one.

Some Cautions About Using Scraps

• Check all scraps for fiber content, color fastness and shrinkage. If you are unsure of a scrap, wash it again.

• Be aware of the grain line in the scrap fabric.

• Rotary cutting scrap fabrics is usually less time and materials efficient than using pieces of yardage.

• Estimate about 20% more scrap fabric for your scrap quilt. You will probably need to edit the fabric requirements given as you work.

Choosing Fabrics for Scrap Quilts

Understanding the underlying structure of a quilt design is especially critical when planning and sewing a scrap quilt. Pay close attention to the placement of light, dark and medium values in a design. Use the following guidelines when positioning your scrap fabrics.

1. The darkest/brightest or lightest/brightest fabrics pull the eye first. Medium/dull fabrics recede, or fill in the design.

2. Warm hues advance—cool hues tend to recede.

3. The more different fabrics you use in a scrap quilt, the less important any one fabric becomes—except those fabrics/values critical to the underlying structure of the quilt design. Be consistent in placing the lightest and darkest fabrics. For example, the structure of the *Trip Around the Scrap Basket*, page 49, is created by the black squares and the muslin bars. These fabrics are the ones that draw the eye. There are hundreds of scrap pieces in the design that are secondary to the black and muslin.

Color Focus in Scrap Quilts

The *Blue Medallion* quilt, page 80, is also a scrap quilt, but one where there is a second focus in the structure of the quilt. The black and muslin still create the frame of the design, but the color blue is the focus hue. There are more blue scraps than other colored scraps.

Using Color and Contrast

You don't have to be an artist to know that color and contrast are important to your quilt making. You can become confident in using contrast and selecting colors and fabrics for your quilts by learning and understanding only a few guidelines.

Although color attracts the eye and sets the mood of the quilt, it is the contrast between the colors used or the lights and darks in the quilt that defines the quilt pattern. For this reason, I believe contrast to be more important than color.

Usually an interesting quilt demonstrates more than one type of contrast. Not only will there be a contrast of colors, but also of print fabrics, color intensity and the use of light and dark areas of the quilt.

Color *value* refers to the amount of light or dark in a color. *Shade* refers to color that is on the darker portion of a scale. *Tint* refers to color that is on the lighter side of a scale. The *pure color* appears in the center of the scale. The most intense bar on the scale is the pure hue at the center. **(Diagram 8)**

| Tints | | Pure Color | | Shades |

Diagram 8

A good way to plan a quilt is to think of the design only in terms of value. **(Diagram 9)** Remember that value/contrast is what makes the quilt design intelligible.

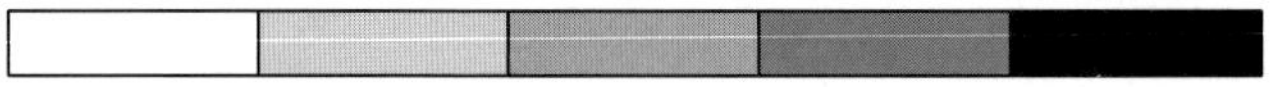

Diagram 9

Effective use of color and contrast is more an art than a science. Quilters will have their personal preference. There are no absolutes when it comes to using color. Harmonies that you will find illustrated on color wheels are helpful starting points for discovering your own preferences, but they are not meant to be rigid rules. The truth is that every color can be made to go with any other color, given the effective use of value and contrast.

BASIC SEWING SUPPLIES

Sewing machine: Use a machine that has a straight stitch capability for all machine piecing.

Machine needles: Use a quilting or sharp embroidery needle for piecing. Change the needle in your machine often.

Hand-sewing needles: Use hand-sewing needles for finishing and detail work. Use a sharp needle for most work and a between needle for hand quilting.

Threads: Use high-quality, 100% cotton or cotton-covered polyester all-purpose threads for machine piecing and finishing.

Seam ripper: Use a sharp seam ripper with a safety tip for removing seams.

Tweezers: Use tweezers to remove pesky threads after seam ripping.

Scissors: Sharp fabric scissors are necessary for trimming fabric, seam allowances and clipping threads.

Marking tools: Removable, light and dark markers for marking dark and light fabrics. Experiment with scraps and markers to determine which tools are best for you.

Rotary tools: Rotary tools include a rotary cutter, extra blades, cutting mat and a 6" x 24" clear acrylic ruler. Other acrylic tools are good to have on hand – 6" x 12", 3" x 12" and 12" x 12". Be sure to discard old, used rotary cutting blades safely.

Stylus or extra-long needle: Use this tool to push fabric toward the sewing machine needle.

Design board: Use a design board for design. Flannel or flannel-back oilcloth placed on wall for planning the layout of quilt units and blocks.

CUTTING YOUR FABRIC

Read through the step-by-step instructions for the quilt you are making. Also, familiarize yourself with the techniques and methods used for your chosen quilt. Cutting the larger pieces needed from any fabric first is a good general practice.

Cut strips selvage to selvage unless using a directional fabric such as a stripe or directional print.

For the purposes of this book, border and binding strips are cut selvage to selvage. *Note: Additional fabric might be required for cutting borders on the straight of the grain along the selvage.* Cut non-directional fabric with a single fold, selvage-to-selvage and wrong sides together. Cut directional fabrics one thickness at a time with the right side up. Cut on the lengthwise, straight, grain for the best results.

Using the Rotary Tools

1. Straighten the grain of the fabric by gently pulling at opposite corners. First pull in one direction and then pull in the other direction.

2. Fold the fabric in half, selvage to selvage with wrong sides together. The fabric should be smooth, flat, and straight for accurate cutting.

3. Place the folded fabric along one of the horizontal lines on the cutting mat. The fabric will extend to the right for right-handed people, or extend to the left for left-handed people. **(Diagram 10)**

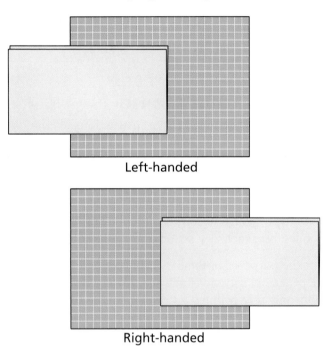

Left-handed

Right-handed

Diagram 10

4. Place the acrylic ruler perpendicular to the folded edge of the fabric. Alternately, use the vertical guidelines on your cutting mat.

5. Trim any rough edges on the fabric.

6. Using the guide marks on the acrylic ruler, measure the required strip to be cut. Rest the open rotary blade flush against the ruler; press down firmly on the mat and begin cutting away from yourself. Cut through the doubled width of fabric in one clean movement. **(Diagram 11)**

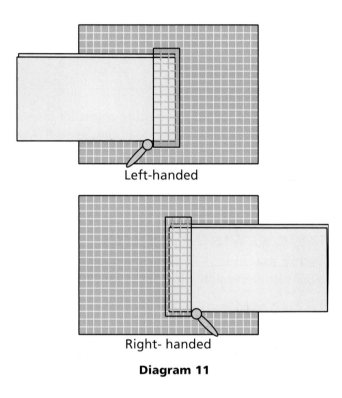

Left-handed

Right- handed

Diagram 11

TIPS

• *After each cut, readjust the ruler and fabric, as needed. Think of a carpenter's tool each time you square up.*

• *Pin a written identification label to all stacks of strips and squares.*

• *Experiment with the number of fabric layers you can cut with accuracy.*

• *Close the rotary cutter after each cut – safety first!*

• *Do not make gestures with an open blade in your hand.*

- *Keep tools away from children, pets – and some husbands.*

- *Use and store mat on a flat surface.*

- *Always measure twice and cut once!*

MAKING THE NINE-PATCH BLOCKS

All of the quilts in this book are created from Nine-Patch blocks. For some of the quilts, it is more practical to construct the blocks one at a time using Traditional Piece-by-Piece Nine-Patch Construction. For many of the quilts, the Strip-Panel Construction is faster and more appropriate.

Notes: All seams are sewn with right sides together using a 1/4" seam allowance.

Traditionally all seams are pressed toward the darker side and all seams are pressed to one side and not open. My practice in pressing machine-sewn seams is to press all seams open.

Traditional Piece-by-Piece Nine-Patch Construction

Use this technique when you want to make one, a few or scrap Nine-Patch blocks.

1. Cut squares for the block the size according to quilt instructions.

2. Lay out the squares in the desired configuration according to the pattern requirements. **(Diagram 12)**

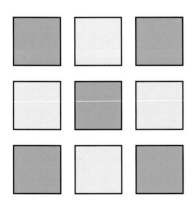

Diagram 12

3. Sew the squares together into units of three. Press. **(Diagram 13)**

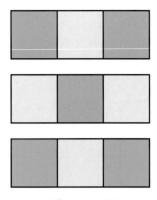

Diagram 13

4. Join these sub-units of squares together. **(Diagram 14)**

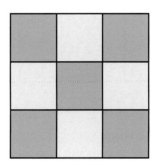

Diagram 14

Strip-Set Panel Nine-Patch Construction

Use this technique when you want to make multiples of the same type Nine-Patch block.

1. Cut fabric strips to size according to quilt instructions.

2. Lay out the strips in the required configuration according to the pattern requirements. Pay close attention to the placement of color and value in each Nine-Patch.

3. For rows 1 and 3, sew the first two strips together using 10 to 12 stitches per inch (2 or 2.5 on some models). **(Diagram 15)** Use a neutral, taupe or medium-beige color thread in the bobbin and on the top to blend with your fabrics. For the best stitches, the color and quality of thread should be the same on the top and in the bobbin.

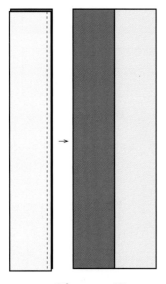

Diagram 15

4. Sew remaining strip to panel to complete strip set. **(Diagram 16)** Sew in the opposite direction of that used in sewing first two strips. Alternating the direction and avoiding pulling at the strips will help avoid bowing and other distortions of the strip-set panels.

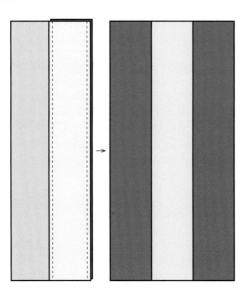

Diagram 16

5. For row 2, sew second strip-set panel in same manner. **(Diagram 17)**

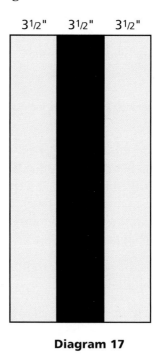

3½"   3½"   3½"

Diagram 17

6. Press strip-set panels using a firm pressing surface or ironing board. A firm surface will result in crisp, sharp seams. A heavily padded surface will not allow proper pressing.

7. Place the strip-set panels on the cutting mat. Trim to create a straight edge. Position the acrylic ruler along one of the horizontal seam lines and measure the required unit width. Make the cut according to the size requirements of the pattern. **(Diagram 18)** Periodically you will need to realign and re-trim the edge.

14

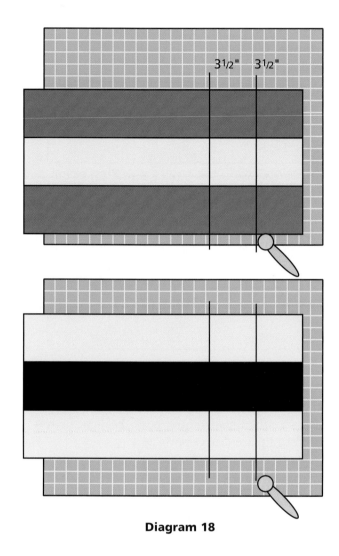

Diagram 18

FINISHING YOUR QUILT

Planning the Finish

Square the quilt blocks or design units to a uniform size. Do not trim away the 1/4" seam allowance.

Pin a note on any block that is undersize. You will need to compensate the seam allowance when joining an undersize block with another block.

Diagonal Sets

Making Side Triangles

The sizes to cut side (setting) triangles are given with individual quilt instructions. If your blocks finish to a different size use the following formula.

1. Take the diagonal measurement of a block or design unit. **(Diagram 20)** Add 2".

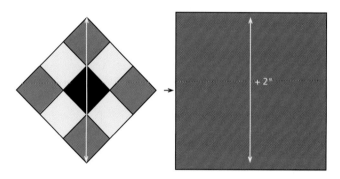

Diagram 20

8. Join sub-units for rows 1, 2 and 3 together to form Nine-Patch block. **(Diagram 19)**

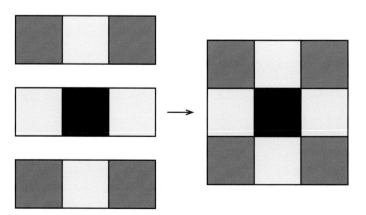

Diagram 19

2. Cut the squares in quarters on the diagonal. **(Diagram 21)**

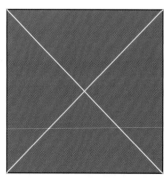

Diagram 21

Making the Corner Triangles

The sizes to cut corner triangles are given with individual quilt instructions. If your blocks finish to a different size use the following formula.

1. Take the measurement of your block or design

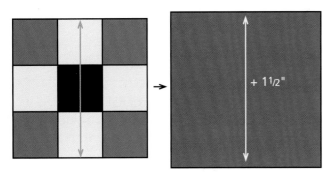

Diagram 22

unit. **(Diagram 22)** Add 1½"

2. Cut the squares in half on the diagonal.

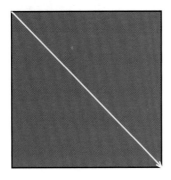

Diagram 23

(Diagram 23)

Sewing the Blocks Together

1. Lay out the blocks and other design elements on a design wall or a large flat surface. Make the final arrangement of the setting according to the quilt design. Sew the rows together.

2. Press the row seams in alternate directions. **(Diagram 24)**

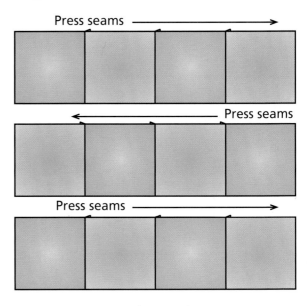

Diagram 24

3. Measure the finished quilt body. Realign the rows or trim to square if necessary.

Adding Borders

After the quilt top is finished and given a final pressing, prepare the top for borders by making sure all corners and sides are straight and square. The top and bottom of the quilt should be the same measurement and the side measurements should be the same.

Trim with rotary tools if necessary, making sure to leave a ¼" seam allowance beyond all pieced points.

If your quilt is larger than the width of the fabric, you will have to piece the border strips. To make longer strips for borders, join two or more cut strips by making a diagonal seam. Trim excess fabric 1/4" from seam and press seam open. **(Diagram 25)**

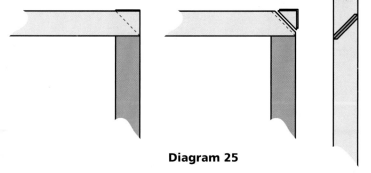

Diagram 25

Simple Borders

1. For the first border (resting strip), cut strips of fabric to match top and bottom quilt measurements. Pin and sew strips to the top and bottom of the quilt.

2. Cut strips of fabric to match the measurement of the sides, including the top and bottom strips. Pin and sew the side strips to the quilt. **(Diagram 26)**

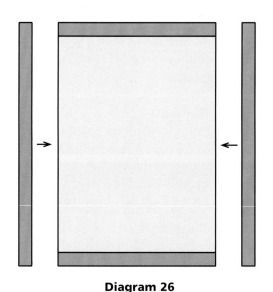

Diagram 26

3. For additional simple borders repeat steps 1 and 2.

Borders with Corner Squares

1. Cut border strips to the top and bottom measurement. Cut two border strips to the true side measurement, before the top and bottom strips are joined to the quilt. **(Diagram 27)**

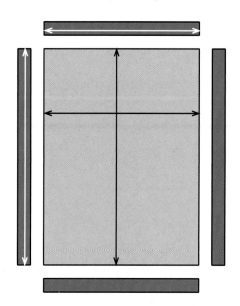

Diagram 27

2. Pin and sew border strips to the top and bottom of the quilt. **(Diagram 28)**

Diagram 28

3. Cut four squares of fabric using the width of the border fabric measurement. For example, a 5"-wide border strip will require a 5" x 5" square. Pieced corner squares can also be used (see the *Dragonfly*, page 84, and *Tuscan Stars*, page 106, quilts).

4. Stitch squares to the ends of the side borders before sewing to the quilt. Finger press the seams toward the border strip.

5. Pin and sew borders to the sides of the quilt matching seams at the corner squares.
(Diagram 29)

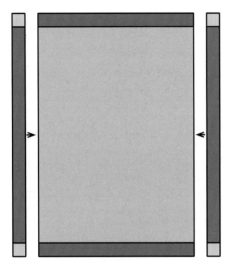

Diagram 29

Layering the Quilt
Backing Fabric
Choose a fabric of similar quality, weight and weave to the quilt top. Select a color that will not show through the batting to the surface of the quilt top. A 100% cotton muslin sheet might be a good backing fabric choice. A 100% cotton percale sheet is not a good choice because of the high thread count.

There was a time when looking at a quilt back meant looking at muslin. Today quilt backs are often as interesting as the surface of the quilt. Experiment! Add some interest to the underside of your quilt by using something bold or by piecing the backing fabric.

Remove the selvages from the backing fabric. Sew sections together, if necessary, to make the backing large enough. Press these seams open. If the seams tend to roll touch the underside with a fabric glue stick to keep them in place and open while you baste and quilt.

The backing and batting should measure 4" to 6" larger than the quilt top. The extra material is needed for shrinkage while quilting or tying and for the outside possibility that the layers will shift while being basted, handled, or quilted.

Batting
There are many types and sizes of batting available for today's quilt maker. There is little problem with fiber migration or bearding with modern battings. Cotton battings are excellent for children's quilts as they have a low incidence of allergic reactions and they burn slowly. Modern wool battings are washable, warm and lightweight. Polyester battings are available in the widest variety of sizes, wash well, and come in various weights and densities.

Buy a good-quality batting from a shop that will discuss the merits of each. Read the content label and quilting or tying requirements for each type of batting you consider. It's a great time to be a quilter— I'm old enough to remember the horrid battings my Grandmother Ritzenthaler had to use!

Take the batting out of the bag and unroll it several hours before you intend to use it. The fibers need to relax and decompress – plump. Use a mist of water on persistent wrinkles.

Layering and Basting
The following information is for quilting or tying the quilt by conventional home methods. Commercial quilting, including long arm quilting machines, will require other methods. Consult the quilting machine operator before proceeding.

1. Place the backing fabric on a large flat surface with the wrong side up – a large table or the floor, if you are agile, are good choices. The floor has advantages: if it is tile, one can tape the backing fabric to

the tile; if it is a carpet, one can straight-pin the backing to the carpet.

2. Center the relaxed batting over the backing. Smooth the batting into place. Pin a few places to keep the two from shifting while you center the top.

3. Press the quilt top. Pre-mark the quilting design. Center the quilt top over the first two layers.

4. Baste the three layers together evenly – about every 6". It's my opinion that one can't baste too much.

5. Quilt by hand or machine.

Tying

If you choose to tie the quilt, use an oversize needle and perle cotton or yarn. Tie about every 4". **(Diagram 30)**

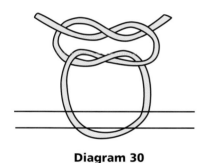

Diagram 30

Making and Applying the Binding

A mitered binding is a good way to put the finishing touches on your quilt. Take your time. It's worth the effort.

1. Place the quilt on a large flat surface and trim excess backing and batting to the edge of the quilt top.

TIP: Slip a large rotary mat under the quilt and use rotary tools to trim – measuring from the seam of the last border.

2. Measure around the outside edges of the quilt. Join binding strips, on the diagonal, to that length. **(Diagram 31)**

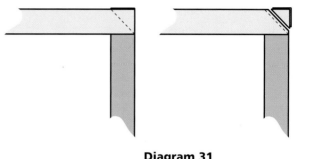

Diagram 31

3. Fold the corner of the binding toward the edge at a 45-degree angle. Press firmly. Trim corner back to a generous 1/4". Fold binding over and press in half with wrong sides together for the entire length. **(Diagram 32)**

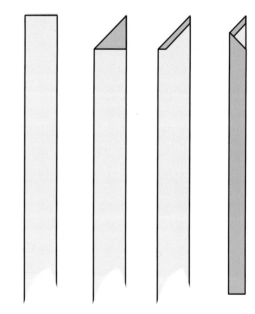

Diagram 32

4. Place folded binding along the edge of the front of the quilted top with raw edges even; begin sewing along one side with a generous 1/4" seam allowance. When you approach to within 1/4" of the corner, stop and pivot to a 45-degree angle; sew to the corner of the quilt. Lift presser foot but do not cut threads. (**Diagram 33**)

5. At the corner, fold the binding at a right angle, 45 degree, away from the quilt top. (**Diagram 34**) Fold back so that the binding is even with the next edge to be stitched. Drop the needle at the corner and continue sewing. (**Diagram 35**) This right angle corner tuck will create a full mitered corner when turned to the wrong side and hand stitched down. Repeat at remaining corners.

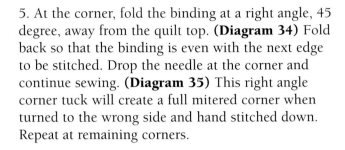

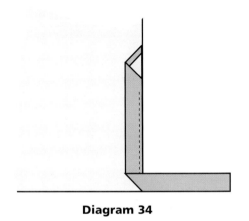

Diagram 34

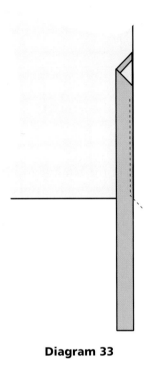

Diagram 33

TIP: If you plan to bind the quilt totally by machine, start by sewing the binding on the wrong side of the quilt and then bringing the binding to the top side for a better machine finish.

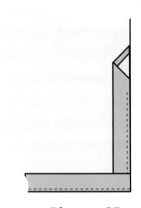

Diagram 35

6. To finish the end of the binding tuck the raw end into the folded end at the beginning of the binding and finish sewing. **(Diagram 36)**

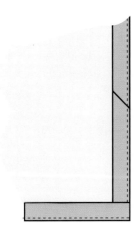

Diagram 36

7. Turn the binding to the opposite side of the quilt and stitch with a hidden stitch. Use a neutral thread. Close the mitered corner tuck with a few additional hand stitches.

Easy Does It

Easy Does It says it all. One of the easiest ways to change a basic Nine-Patch block into something more interesting is to "snowball" the corners. Diagonally sew squares onto the corners of the basic Nine-Patch to soften, or round, their appearance—thus the term "snowball."

In this quilt you see five Nine Patches changed into traditional Shoo-fly blocks by snowballing and four basic Nine-Patches used as alternate blocks. The quilt has a charming traditional appearance that would add warmth to any home environment.

Approximate Size: 39" x 39"
Nine Nine-Patch Starter Blocks: 9" finished
Block Size: 9" finished

MATERIALS

Note: Fabric quantities specified are for 42"/44"-wide, 100% cotton fabrics. All measurements include a 1/4-inch seam allowance unless otherwise specified in the instructions. Sew with right sides together unless otherwise stated. Press between each sewing step.

Blocks
3/4 yard assorted light fabrics
5 strips assorted dark prints, 3 1/2" x 22"

Borders and Binding
1/4 yard pink fabric, first border
1 yard print, second border and binding

Backing and Batting
1 1/4 yards backing fabric

CUTTING

Nine-Patch Shoo-Fly Blocks
40 assorted light squares, 3 1/2" x 3 1/2"
5 squares each of five dark prints, 3 1/2" x 3 1/2"

Alternate Blocks
36 light squares, 3 1/2" x 3 1/2"

Borders and Binding
4 light squares, 2" x 2", first border
4 pink strips, 2" x width of fabric, first border
4 print strips, 5" x width of fabric, second border
4 print strips, 2 1/2" x width of fabric, binding

INSTRUCTIONS

Note: Refer to Traditional Piece-by-Piece Nine-Patch Construction, page 13, to make Nine-Patch blocks.

1. Make five Nine-Patch A using the assorted dark print and light squares and four Nine-Patch B using only light squares. (**Diagram 1**)

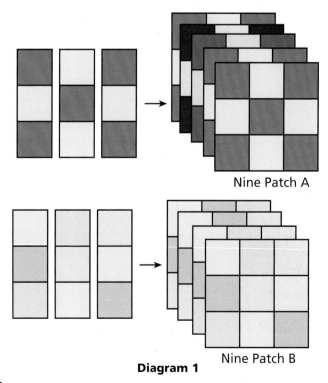

Nine Patch A

Nine Patch B

Diagram 1

2. Place a 3½" light square over a dark print corner of Nine-Patch A. *Note: The light square will be larger than the darker square.* Diagonally sew the squares onto the corners of the Nine-Patch. (**Diagram 2**) *Hint: Draw a line diagonally on wrong side of 3½" light squares.*

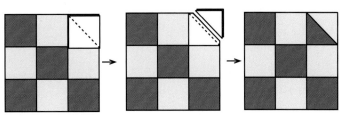

Diagram 2

3. Press the corner back and trim the underside leaving a ¼" seam allowance. Repeat steps 2 and 3 at remaining corners to complete Shoo-fly Block. (**Diagram 3**) Repeat for remaining four Nine-Patch A.

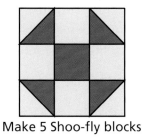

Make 5 Shoo-fly blocks

Diagram 3

4. Square by trimming the blocks to 9½".

OTHER SIZES

	Baby/ Small Lap	Twin	Full/Queen	King
Nine Patch Blocks	8 Shoo-Fly 7 Alternating	32 Shoo-Fly 31 Alternating	50 Shoo Fly 49 Alternating	61 Shoo Fly 60 Alternating
Blocks Set	3 x 5	7 x 9	9 x 11	11 x 11
Size (no borders)	27" x 45"	63" x 81"	81" x 99"	99" x 99"
First Border Strips With Corner Squares	3 @ 2" x width with 4 corner squares Adds 3"	8 @ 2" x width with 4 corner squares Adds 3"	10 @ 2" x width with 4 corner squares Adds 3"	11 @ 2" x width with 4 corner squares Adds 3"
Second Border Strips	4 @ 6" x width Adds 11"	9 @ 3½" x width Adds 6"	11 @ 3½" x width Adds 6"	11 @ 3½" x width Adds 6"
Binding Strips	5 @ 2½" x width	9 @ 2½" x width	11 @ 2½" x width	12 @ 2½" x width
Finished Size	41" x 59"	72" x 90"	90" x 108"	108" x 108"

Yardage

	Baby/ Small Lap	Twin	Full/Queen	King
Assorted Dark Prints	8 strips 3½" x 22"	16 strips 3½" x 44"	25 strips 3½" x 44"	32 Strips 3½" x 44"
Assorted Light Prints	¾ yard	5 yards	7½ yards	9½ yards
First Border Pink	¼ yard	½ yard	¾ yard	¾ yard
Second Border and Binding	1¼ yards	1⅝ yards	1⅞ yards	2¼ yards

Quilt Assembly

1. Place quilt blocks in three horizontal rows of three blocks each—alternating the Shoo-Fly and Nine-Patch B blocks. (**Diagram 4**)

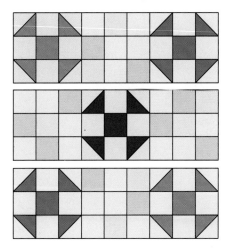

Diagram 4

2. Join the blocks in each row together.

3. Join the rows.

Note: *Refer to Adding the Borders, page 16, for borders.*

4. For first border, measure the sides of the quilt and cut four 2" pink strips to this measurement.

5. Sew a pink strip to the top and bottom of the quilt.

6. Sew a 2" x 2" light square to the ends of the remaining two pink strips. Join these strips to the sides of the quilt. (**Diagram 5**)

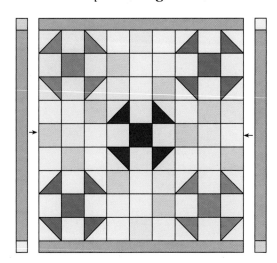

Diagram 5

7. For second border, measure across top and bottom of quilt. Cut two 5" print strips to this measurement and sew to top and bottom of quilt. Measure length of quilt. Cut two 5" print strips to this measurement and sew to sides of quilt.

8. Layer top, batting and backing and quilt as desired.

9. Make 4½ yards of straight grain binding. See General Directions, page 19, for making and applying binding.

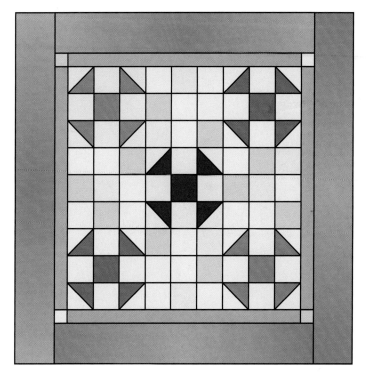

Easy Does It Quilt Layout

25

Jelly Beans

The fabrics in a Nine-Patch block are arranged any number of ways. This quilt uses two types of very different Starter Blocks. Like most other things in quilt making—things always are better when shared.

Approximate Size: 49" x 49"
16 Starter Nine-Patch Blocks: 9" finished
Jelly Bean Block Size: 8" finished

MATERIALS

Note: Fabric quantities specified are for 42"/44"-wide, 100% cotton fabrics. All measurements include a 1/4-inch seam allowance unless otherwise specified in the instructions. Sew with right sides together unless otherwise stated. Press between each sewing step.

Blocks and Borders

Approximately 1 yard scraps of bright, jelly bean-colored fabric, blocks
1/2 yard white fabric, blocks
12 bright fabric strips, 3 1/2" x 16 1/2", sashing
4 bright fabric strips, 4 1/2" x width of fabric, border

Binding

1/2 yard

Note: Photographed quilt is made from assorted bright strips sewn in a long continuous strip.

Batting and Backing

2 1/2 yards backing fabric
Batting, size to fit

CUTTING

Note: To make best use of your fabrics cut in the order given.

Blocks

104 assorted bright fabric squares, 3 1/2" x 3 1/2"
4 white fabric strips, 3 1/2" x width of fabric
Cut into 40 squares, 3 1/2" x 3 1/2"

Sashing, Border and Binding

9 assorted bright squares, 3 1/2" x 3 1/2", sashing corners
12 assorted bright strips, 3 1/2" x 16 1/2", sashing strips
4 assorted bright strips, 4 1/2" x width, border
4 bright fabric squares, 4 1/2" x 4 1/2, border corners
6 binding strips, 2 1/2" x width (or several assorted bright strips to equal length)

INSTRUCTIONS

The Blocks

Note: Refer to Traditional Piece-by-Piece Nine-Patch Construction, page 13, to make Nine-Patch blocks.

1. Sew a 3½" white square to opposite sides of a 3½" bright square; repeat. Sew a 3½" bright square to opposite sides of a 3½" white square. Sew rows together for Nine-Patch A. (**Diagram 1**) Make eight Nine-Patch A.

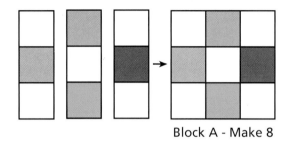

Block A - Make 8

Diagram 1

2. Sew three assorted 3½" bright squares together; repeat two more times. Sew rows together for Nine-Patch B. (**Diagram 2**) Make eight Nine-Patch B.

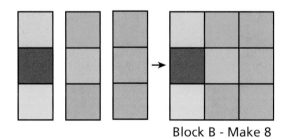

Block B - Make 8

Diagram 2

3. Measuring from the inside seam, slice through the blocks at 1½"; continue all around the block, **Diagram 3.** Cut only one block at a time. **Caution:** *Cut very carefully.*

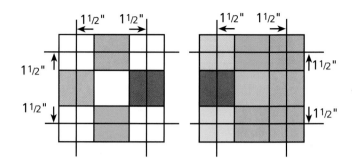

Diagram 3

4. Cut all Nine-Patch A blocks and separate the parts. Cut all Nine-Patch B blocks and separate the parts. (**Diagram 4**)

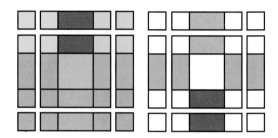

Diagram 4

5. Put all the A centers and corners together; put all the B centers and corners together. (**Diagram 5**)

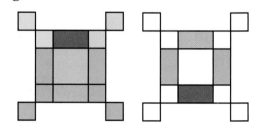

Diagram 5

6. Exchange the side strips from the two blocks. (**Diagram 6**)

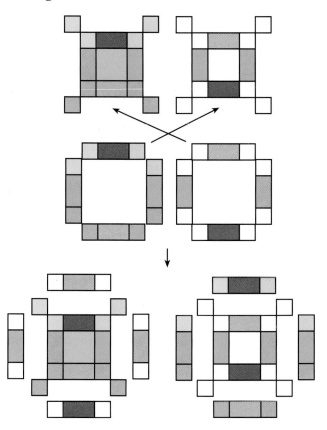

Diagram 6

7. For each block, sew strips to top and bottom of block. Sew corner squares to side strips and sew to block. (**Diagram 7**) Continue with all remaining Nine-Patch blocks. You will have eight blocks with white centers and eight with bright centers.

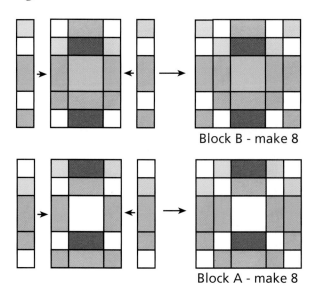

Block B - make 8

Block A - make 8

Diagram 7

Quilt Assembly

1. Join a Block A and block B; repeat. Sew pairs together. (**Diagram 8**) Make four sections.

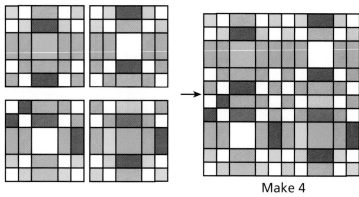

Make 4

Diagram 8

2. Square by trimming the sections to $16\frac{1}{2}$".

3. Sew three $3\frac{1}{2}$" bright sashing strips and two pieced sections together; repeat. (**Diagram 9**)

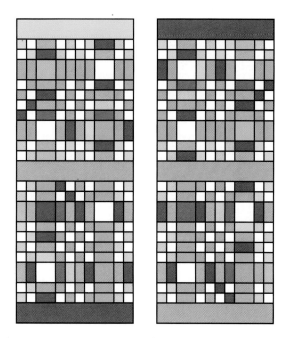

Diagram 9

29

4. Sew three 3½" bright sashing squares and two 3½" bright 3½" x 16½" sashing strips together; repeat two more times. (**Diagram 10**)

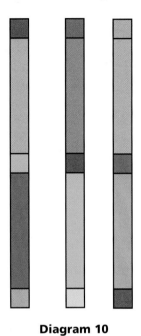

Diagram 10

5. Sew all rows together. (**Diagram 11**)

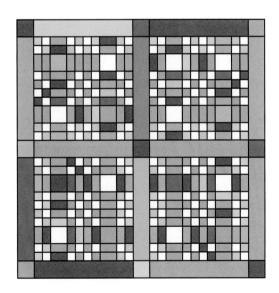

Diagram 11

Note: *Refer to Borders with Corner Squares, page 17, for adding the border with cornerstones.*

6. Measure the quilt in both directions and cut four 4½" bright strips to fit the sides. Sew strips to top and bottom. Sew a 4½" bright square to each end of remaining strips and sew to sides to complete quilt. (**Diagram 12**)

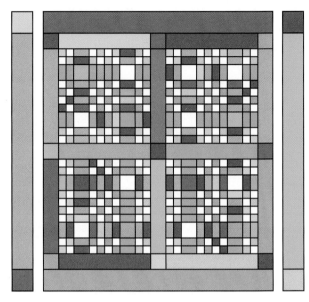

Diagram 12

7. Layer top, batting and backing and quilt as desired.

8. Make 5 yards of straight grain binding. See General Directions, page 19, for making and applying binding.

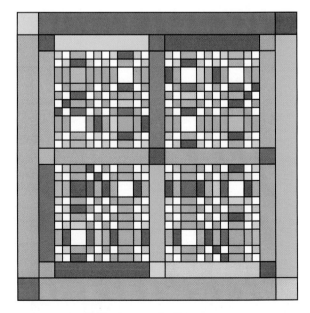

Jelly Beans Quilt Layout

Scrap Bag Shadow Boxes

Anything goes – is the theme for this scrap quilt. You can't go wrong as long as you select fabric with adequate contrast. For the most effective scrap quilt choose a wide variety of fabric colors and patterns.

Approximate Size: 61" x 84"
16 Starter Nine-Patch Blocks: 9" finished
Block Size: 11" finished

MATERIALS

Note: Fabric quantities specified are for 42"/44"- wide, 100% cotton fabrics. If making a scrap quilt choose fabric equivalent to the amounts given below. Read ahead to the measurements given under Cutting. All measurements include a 1/4-inch seam allowance unless otherwise specified in the instructions. Sew with right sides together unless otherwise stated. Press between each sewing step.

Shadow Boxes
1 1/8 yards black fabric
1 3/4 yards assorted medium/bright prints
1 yard assorted light fabrics

Large Triangles
1 yard assorted light fabrics
1 yard assorted dark bright fabrics

Pieced Border
Small Nine Patches
1 1/2 yards light fabric
3/4 yard assorted medium dark bright prints

Second Border and Binding
3 yards large print

Backing and Batting
4 3/4 yards
Twin-size batting

CUTTING

Shadow Box Blocks
6 black strips, 3 1/2" x width
8 assorted medium bright print strips, 3 1/2" x width
4 light fabric strips, 3 1/2" x width
18 light fabric squares, 6 1/2" x 6 1/2". (Cut in half on the diagonal.)
14 assorted dark bright print squares, 6 1/2" x 6 1/2" (Cut in half on the diagonal.)

Pieced Border and Binding
16 assorted light squares, 7 1/16" x 7 1/16", pieced border
8 medium dark bright strips, 1 7/8" x width of fabric, pieced border
7 light strips, 1 7/8" x width of fabric, pieced border
7 large print strips, 7 3/4" x width of fabric, second border
8 large print strips, 2 1/2" x width of fabric, binding

INSTRUCTIONS

Shadow Box Blocks

Note: Refer to Strip-Set Panel Nine-Patch Construction, page 13, to make Nine-Patch blocks.

1. Sew a 3½" medium bright strip to each side of a 3½" light fabric strip; cut at 3½" intervals. (**Diagram 1**)

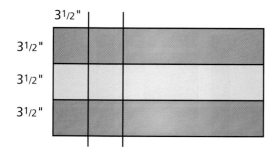

Diagram 1

2. Sew a 3½" light fabric strip to each side of a 3½" black strip; cut at 3½" intervals. (**Diagram 2**)

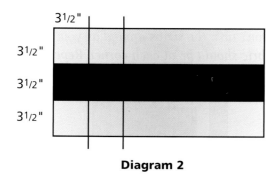

Diagram 2

3. Sew sub-units together to form Nine-Patch A. (**Diagram 3**) Make eight Nine-Patch A.

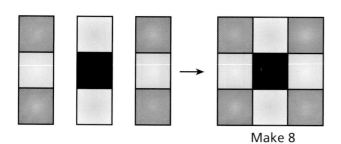

Make 8

Diagram 3

4. Sew a 3½" black strip to each side of a 3½" medium bright strip; cut at 3½" intervals. (**Diagram 4**)

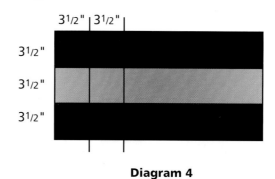

Diagram 4

5. Sew a 3½" medium bright strip to each side of a 3½" black strip; cut at 3½" intervals. (**Diagram 5**)

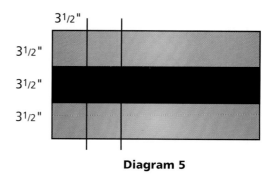

Diagram 5

6. Sew sub-units together to form Nine-Patch B. (**Diagram 6**) Make eight Nine-Patch B.

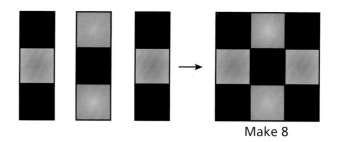

Make 8

Diagram 6

7. Pair one A block with one B block.

Caution: *Work only with two blocks at a time.*

3. Lay out the blocks in five rows of three alternating the background fabrics. (**Diagram 15**)

Diagram 15

4. Sew together in rows. Sew the rows together.

5. Sew a 1⅞" medium bright strip to each side of a light fabric; cut at 1⅞" intervals. (**Diagram 16**)

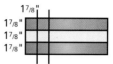

Diagram 16

6. Sew a 1⅞" light fabric strip to each side of a 1⅞" medium bright strip; cut at 1⅞" intervals. (**Diagram 17**)

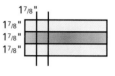

Diagram 17

7. Sew sub-units from steps 5 and 6 together to make small Nine-Patch blocks. (**Diagram 18**) Make 36 small Nine-Patch blocks.

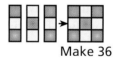

Make 36

Diagram 18

8. Cut the 16 light 7¹/₁₆" x 7¹/₁₆" squares diagonally into quarters. (**Diagram 19**)

Diagram 19

9. Sew light triangles to opposite sides of a Nine-Patch block. Make 12 each of type, A and B. (**Diagram 20**)

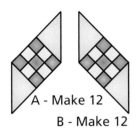

A - Make 12
B - Make 12

Diagram 20

10. Make four each of type, C and D. (**Diagrams 21 and 22**)

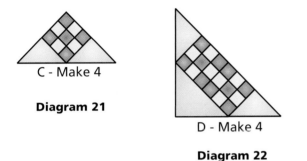

C - Make 4

Diagram 21

D - Make 4

Diagram 22

11. Look at **Diagram 23.** Assemble the top and bottom strips using C units, A units and B units. Sew to the quilt.

Diagram 23

12. Assemble the pieced sides of the quilt with C units, A units and B units. Sew to the sides of the quilt.

13. Add the D units to the corners of the quilt.

Note: *Refer to Adding Borders, page 16, to add the final border.*

14. Measure across top and bottom of quilt. Cut two 7³/4" medium bright strips to this measurement and sew to top and bottom of quilt. Measure quilt lengthwise. Cut two 7³/4" medium bright strips to this measurement and sew to sides of quilt.

Layout

15. Layer top, batting and backing and quilt as desired.

16. Make 8 yards of straight grain binding. See General Directions, page 19, for making and applying binding.

Scrap Bag Shadow Boxes Quilt 2

This quilt shows the Scrap Bag Shadow Boxes using different fabrics in a slightly different arrangement. A large floral print replaces the leafy batik print. Use the same yardage and cutting requirements given on page 31, noting the positions of the light and dark fabrics.

The Village

An old African proverb, "It takes a village to raise a child," is a concept that should apply to all cultures and for all ages of human kind. Our villages should help care for our young, our elderly – all of our people. This quilt effectively uses scraps to create fun, colorful, or beautiful quilts for all those in our cities, towns and villages needing them.

Approximate Size: 40³/4" x 56¹/4"
Six Nine-Patch Starter Blocks: 15¹/2" finished
Design Unit Size: 7³/4" finished

MATERIALS

Note: *Fabric quantities specified are for 42"/44"-wide, 100% cotton fabrics. All measurements include a ¹/4-inch seam allowance unless otherwise specified in the instructions. Sew with right sides together unless otherwise stated. Press between each sewing step.*

Blocks
1 yard vivid print fabric (the photographed quilt uses ¹/4 yard each of four different prints)
³/4 yard blue fabric
¹/8 yard golden yellow fabric

Borders and Binding
³/4 yard print, border
¹/2 yard print, binding*
* *Photographed quilt does not have a separate binding. The polar fleece backing is folded toward the front and stitched down.)*

Backing
1³/4 yards polar fleece

I have been the teaching guest of many guilds whose members are actively making thousands of quilts for children in crisis, AIDS patients, the elderly, and those in hospice care. There are countless organizations benefiting from this loving concern and activity.

After one such trip, I went straight to my stash and pulled fabric for a "Hide-n-Seek" quilt for my Mother who was, at that time, in a care center. She delighted in spying every type of cat, bug, and spider I had pieced into her quilt.

This quilt uses the same concept of self-sashing blocks used for my Mothers quilt. There is a big difference. Because the Starter Nine-Patch block is larger, constructing the quilt is much faster.

CUTTING

Nine-Patch Starter Blocks

24 vivid print squares, $6^{1/2}$" x $6^{1/2}$"

24 blue rectangles, $4^{1/2}$" x $6^{1/2}$"

6 golden yellow squares, $4^{1/2}$" x $4^{1/2}$"

Side Units

6 blue rectangles, $4^{1/2}$" x $6^{1/2}$"

3 golden yellow squares, $4^{1/2}$" x $4^{1/2}$"

1 golden yellow square, $2^{1/4}$" x $2^{1/4}$"

Border

4 vivid print squares, $4^{1/2}$" x $4^{1/2}$"

5 print strips, $4^{1/2}$" x width of fabric

Binding

5 print strips, $2^{1/2}$" x width of fabric

INSTRUCTIONS

Note: Refer to Traditional Piece-by-Piece Nine-Patch Construction, page 13, to make Nine-Patch blocks.

1. Sew a $6^{1/2}$" vivid print square to opposite sides of a $4^{1/2}$" x $6^{1/2}$" blue rectangle; repeat. Sew a $4^{1/2}$" x $6^{1/2}$" blue rectangle to opposite sides of a $4^{1/2}$" golden yellow square. Sew rows together to complete Nine-patch block. **(Diagram 1)** Make six nine-Patch blocks.

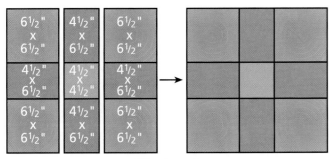

Diagram 1

2. Cut each Nine-Patch block into equal quarters. Measure 2" from the seam line when cutting. **(Diagram 2)** This will make 24 design units each measuring $8^{1/4}$" x $8^{1/4}$".

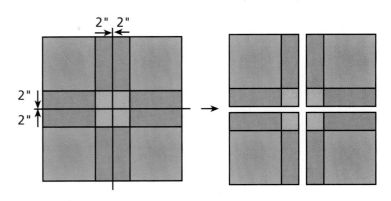

Diagram 2

3. Square the design units to $8^{1/4}$" x $8^{1/4}$".

Quilt Assembly

1. Arrange the design units into a pleasing arrangement. All the golden yellow squares should be facing down and to the left as you view them. Join the blocks in each row together. Join the rows. **(Diagram 3)**

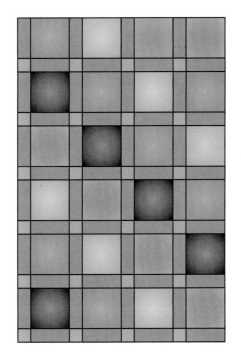

Diagram 3

41

2. To complete the top and right side of the quilt body, sew a 4½" x 6½" blue rectangle to opposite sides of a 4½" golden yellow square; repeat two more times. Sub-cut into quarters. **(Diagram 4)**

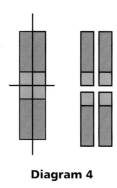

Diagram 4

3. Join four quarter-units and sew to top of the quilt. Sew six quarter-units and one 2¼" golden yellow square and sew to right side of quilt, **Diagram 5.**

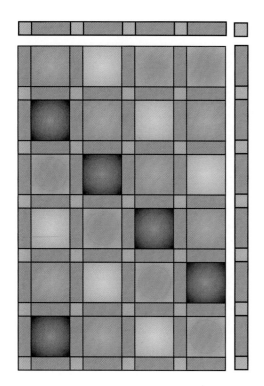

Diagram 5

Note: Refer to Borders with Corner Squares, page 17, to add border.

4. Measure across the top and bottom of the quilt. Cut two 4½" print strips to this measurement. Measure the length of the quilt and cut two 4½" print strips to this measurement.

5. Sew border strips to the top and bottom of the quilt. Sew two 4½" x 4½" vivid print squares to each end of the two remaining border strips. Sew to the sides of the quilt.

6. Center and layer the top and backing.

Note: Be sure backing is at least 2" larger than the quilt top on all four sides.

7. Tie the top and backing together with embroidery floss or other lightweight cording. See General Directions, page 19, for tying.

8. Trim the backing to 1" from the body of the quilt.

9. Roll the fleece from back to front and stitch the edge to the front of the quilt by hand or machine.

The Village Quilt Layout

42

Lattice

The diagonal set used for this quilt is an excellent method of displaying favorite fabrics or colors in a quilt. It's a wonderful quilt design for pulling together a decorating or color theme.

Approximate Size: 52" x 66"
Ten Nine-Patch Starter Blocks: 11" finished
Design Unit Size: 5^1/4" finished

MATERIALS

Note: Fabric quantities specified are for 42"/44"-wide, 100% cotton fabrics. All measurements include a ^{1}/4-inch seam allowance unless otherwise specified in the instructions. Sew with right sides together unless otherwise stated. Press between each sewing step.

Blocks and Body of Quilt

^{1}/2 yard muslin
^{1}/4 yard red, cornerstones
^{3}/4 yard co-ordinating fabric
   *Scrap Technique: Plan ^{1}/8 yard each –
   after washing and trimming – of five
   co-ordinating fabrics.*
^{1}/2 yard medium print, finishing triangles

Borders

^{1}/2 yard plaid
^{7}/8 yard yellow print
1^1/2 yards red print

Backing and Batting

3^1/4 yards backing fabric
Twin-size batting

DIAGONAL SET QUILTS
When blocks or design units are placed on point, it is a "diagonal set." There are two secrets to successful diagonal set quilts.

1. Cut oversize finishing triangles maintaining the straight of the grain on the outside edges of the triangles. These are trimmed after the body of the quilt is complete.

2. Lay out the quilt with the design units and finishing triangles before you begin sewing the top together.

**SPECIAL NOTES FOR
THE LATTICE QUILT**
1. In addition to the finishing triangles there are small finishing units that complete the lattice at the outer edges of the quilt. These are either sewn to the end of a diagonal row or to a finishing triangle.

2. The quilt is assembled in two halves. Rows one through four are sewn first – in order. Rows five through nine are sewn together – in that order.

3. The corner triangles are sewn on last.

CUTTING

Nine-Patch Starter Blocks & Body of Quilt

3 muslin strips, 4½" x width of fabric

2 red strips, 3½" x width of fabric

1 muslin strip, 3½" x width of fabric

5 coordinating fabric strips, 4½" x width of fabric

4 medium print squares, 9" x 9" (Resulting triangles will be slightly oversized.)

2 medium print squares, 6" x 6" (Resulting triangles will be slightly oversized.)

1 red square, 1¾"' x 1¾"

Borders

5 plaid strips, 3" x width of fabric (first border)

4 red squares, 3" x 3" (first border cornerstones)

5 yellow print strips, 4" x width of fabric (second border)

6 red print strips, 5" x width of fabric (third border)

Binding

6 red print strips, 2½" x width of fabric

INSTRUCTIONS

Design Units

Note: *Refer to Strip-Set Panel Nine-Patch Construction, page 13, to make Nine-Patch blocks.*

1. Sew 4½" coordinating print strip to each side of 3½" muslin strip. Cut strip set at 4½" intervals for a total of 20 sub-units. (**Diagram 1**)

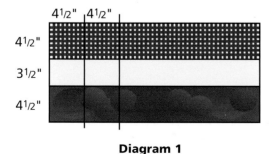

Diagram 1

2. Sew 4½" muslin strip to each side of 3½" red strip. Cut at 3½" intervals for a total of 10 sub-units. (**Diagram 2**)

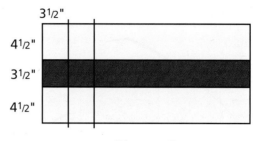

Diagram 2

3. Sew sub-units to form Nine-Patch. (**Diagram 3**) Make ten Nine-Patch Blocks.

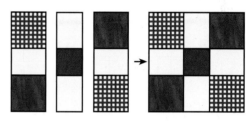

Diagram 3

4. Cut each Nine-Patch block into equal quarters. Measure 1½" from the seam line when cutting. (**Diagram 4**)

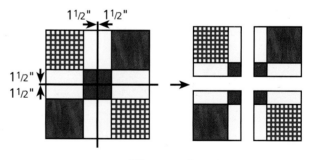

Diagram 4

5. Square the resulting design units by trimming to 5¾" x 5¾".

Quilt Assembly

1. For finishing (setting) triangles, cut the four 9" x 9" medium print squares into quarters on the diagonal. For corner triangles, cut the two 6" x 6" squares in half on the diagonal. (**Diagram 5**)

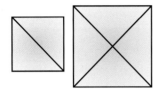

Diagram 5

2. From the leftover muslin/red strip sets from the Nine-Patch construction, cut five sub-units. Quarter-cut these units. (**Diagram 6**)

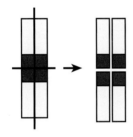

Diagram 6

3. Sew sub-units to finishing triangles to make eight A finishing units and five B finishing units. (**Diagram 7**)

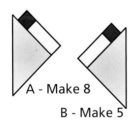

A - Make 8
B - Make 5

Diagram 7

Note: The remaining quarter-cut sub-units are used to finish some of the diagonal rows. See the quilt layout for the exact placement.

4. Lay out the design units and all the finishing sub-units and triangles. (**Diagram 8**)

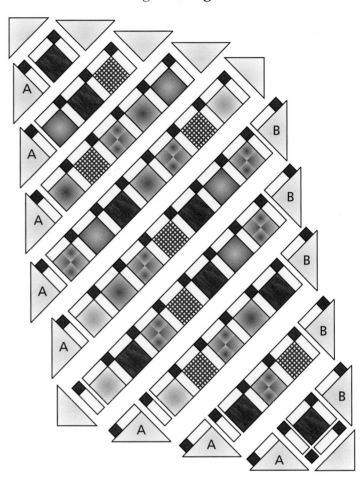

Diagram 8

5. Sew the design units together in rows. Add the finishing triangles and finishing units.

6. Pin together rows one through four to match seams. Sew rows together. (**Diagram 9**)

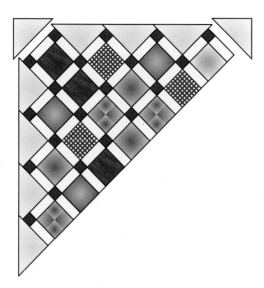

Diagram 9

7. Pin together rows five through nine to match seams. Sew rows together. (**Diagram 10**)

Diagram 10

8. Join the two halves together. (**Diagram 11**)

Diagram 11

9. Trim the body of the quilt. Leave a ¼" seam allowance on the outside point of the red cornerstones. (**Diagram 12**)

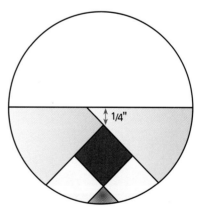

1/4"

Diagram 12

Note: *Refer to Adding Borders, page 16, to add borders.*

10. For first border, measure top and bottom of the quilt. Cut two 3" plaid strips to this measurement. Measure the sides of the quilt and cut two 3" plaid strips to this measurement.

11. Sew the top and bottom strips to the quilt. Sew 3" red squares to each end of the two remaining border strips and sew the side borders to the quilt.

12. For second border, measure across top and bottom of the quilt. Cut two 4" yellow print border strips to that length and sew to top and bottom of quilt. Measure length of quilt. Cut two 4" yellow print strips to that length and sew to sides of quilt.

13. Repeat step 3 for third border using 5" red print strips.

14. Layer top, batting and backing and quilt as desired.

15. Make 6 yards of straight grain binding. See General Directions, page 19, for making and applying binding.

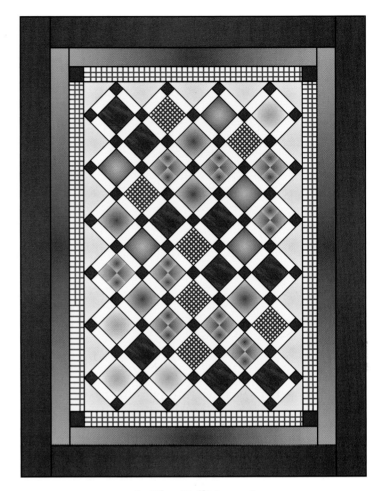

Lattice Quilt Layout

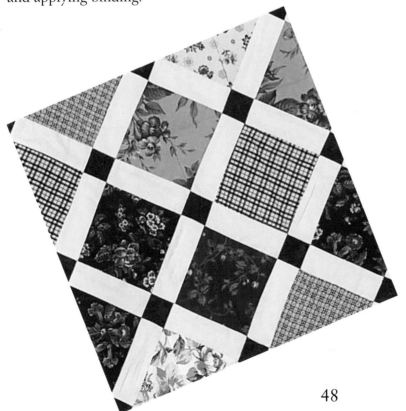

Trip Around the Scrap Basket

The traditional Trip Around the World setting gets a new look with these scrappy little units cut from Nine-Patch blocks. Look closely and you can see that I dug deeply into the scrap boxes for this quilt.

Approximate Size: 40" x 56"
13 Nine-Patch Starter Blocks: 9" finished
Design Unit Size: 4" finished

MATERIALS

Note: Fabric quantities specified are for 42"/44"-wide, 100% cotton fabrics. All measurements include a 1/4-inch seam allowance unless otherwise specified in the instructions. Sew with right sides together unless otherwise stated. Press between each sewing step.

Blocks

1/4 yard black fabric
2 yards assorted scrap print fabrics
   (more will give you a greater variety)
3/4 yard muslin

Border and Binding

1 yard stripe fabric

Backing and Batting

3 yards backing fabric
Twin-size batting

CUTTING

Nine-Patch Starter Blocks

10 assorted print strips, 3 1/2" x 22"
5 muslin strips, 3 1/2" x 22"
4 muslin strips, 3 1/2" x width of fabric
2 black strips, 3 1/2" x width of fabric

> **SCRAP QUILT TIP**
> The use of black and muslin fabrics repeated in the same position in this quilt keep the design recognizable as a Trip Around the World. They constitute the framework of the pattern. They are the darkest and the lightest fabrics in the quilt—the eye will naturally seek the darkest and lightest values.

Design Units

52 assorted print squares, 4 3/4" x 4 3/4"
   Hint: It's more interesting if these fabrics are different from those used in the Nine-Patch blocks.

Border and Binding

5 stripe fabric strips, 4 3/4" x width of fabric, border
5 stripe fabric strips, 2 1/2" x width of fabric, binding

INSTRUCTIONS

Note: Refer to Strip-Set Panel Nine-Patch Construction, page 13, to make Nine-Patch blocks.

1. Sew a 3¹/2" x 22" print strip to each side of a 3¹/2" x 22" muslin strip; repeat with another set of colors. Sew a 3¹/2" muslin strip to each side of a 3¹/2" black strip. Cut strip sets at 3¹/2" intervals. (**Diagram 1**)

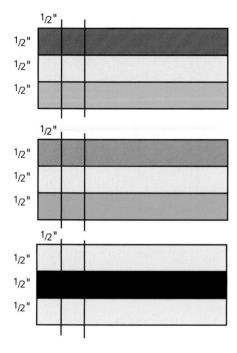

Diagram 1

2. Sew sub-units together to form Nine-Patch block. (**Diagram 2**) Make 13 Nine-Patch blocks.

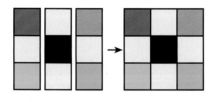

Diagram 2

3. Cut each Nine-Patch block into equal quarters. Measure 1¹/2" from the seam line when cutting. This will make 52 quarters each measuring 4³/4" x 4³/4". (**Diagram 3**)

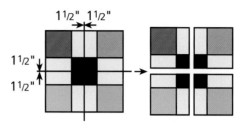

Diagram 3

Note: *The following steps reveal the secret to this wonderfully scrappy Trip Around the World quilt.*

4. Mark a diagonal pencil line on the wrong side of every quarter-unit. Mark from light corner to light corner. (**Diagram 4**)

 Diagram 4

5. Place a 4³/4" print square right sides together with a quarter-unit. Using the pencil line as a guide, sew ¹/8" on each side of the line. (**Diagram 5**)

 Diagram 5

6. Cut the quarter-unit in half along the diagonal pencil line. Press this small seam towards the larger triangular piece. This step results in two design units–A and B. (**Diagram 6**)

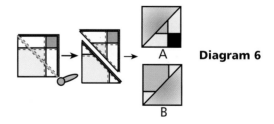 **Diagram 6**

7. Square units by trimming to 4¹/2" x 4¹/2".

51

Quilt Assembly

1. Arrange 96 design units (you will have four left over) into the Trip Around the World pattern. Lay them out into quarter sections, each 4 x 6 units. (**Diagram 7**)

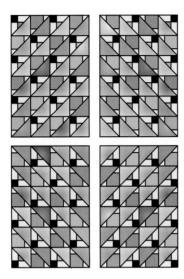

Diagram 7

2. Join the blocks in each row together. Join the rows.

3. Sew the quarter sections together. (**Diagram 8**)

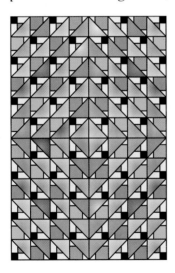

Diagram 8

Note: *Refer to Borders with Corner Squares, page 17, to add border with corners.*

4. Measure across top and bottom of quilt and cut two 4³/4" stripe strips to this measurement. Measure length of quilt and cut two 4³/4" stripe strip to this measurement.

5. Sew a border strip to the top and bottom of the quilt.

6. Sew a quarter-unit to the ends of the two remaining border strips. Join these strips to the sides of the quilt. (**Diagram 9**)

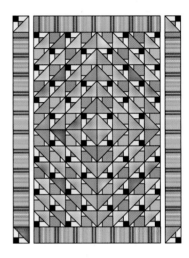

Diagram 9

7. Layer top, batting and backing and quilt as desired.

8. Make 5¹/2 yards of straight grain binding. See General Directions, page 19, for making and applying binding.

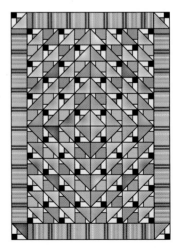

Trip Around the Scrap Basket Quilt Layout

Arizona Road Trip

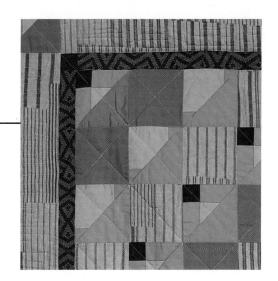

Take a trip on Route 66 where you will observe similar colors and graphic shapes in the art of the American West.

Approximate Size: 43" x 59"
Seven Nine-Patch Starter Blocks:
  9" finished
Design Unit Size: 4" finished

MATERIALS

Note: Fabric quantities specified are for 42"/44"-wide, 100% cotton fabrics. All measurements include a 1/4-inch seam allowance unless otherwise specified in the instructions. Sew with right sides together unless otherwise stated. Press between each sewing step.

Blocks
  1/8 yard dark red fabric
  1/4 yard gray blue fabric
  1/3 yard turquoise fabric
  1/3 yard dusty rose fabric
  1/2 yard sage green fabric
  5/8 yard terra cotta fabric
  5/8 yard coordinating stripe fabric

Borders and Binding
  1/4 yard red violet fabric, first border
  2 yards stripe fabric, second border

Backing and Batting
  2 3/4 yards backing fabric
  Batting, size to fit

USING STRIPED FABRIC

- Pay special attention to the direction of the stripes when planning, cutting and sewing.

- More fabric is required for the border in this quilt. The sides are cut on the lengthwise grain, while the top and bottom are cut on the crosswise grain.

- Notice that the stripes in the body of the quilt are going the same direction as those in the outside border.

CUTTING
Nine-Patch Starter Blocks
  4 dusty rose strips, 3 1/2" x width of fabric
  1 dark red strip, 3 1/2" x width of fabric
  4 turquoise strips, 3 1/2" x width of fabric

Design Units
  4 terra cotta squares, 4 3/4" x 4 3/4"
  24 sage green squares, 4 3/4" x 4 3/4"

Plain Blocks

24 terra cotta squares, 4³/4" x 4³/4"

28 co-ordinating stripe squares, 4³/4" x 4³/4"

8 gray blue squares, 4¹/2" x 4¹/2"

Borders and Binding

5 red violet strips, 2" x width of fabric, first border

4 red squares, 2" x 2", first border cornerstones

2 strips, stripe fabric, 4¹/2" x width of fabric, second border

2 strips, stripe fabric, 4¹/2" x length of fabric, second border

5 strips, stripe fabric, 2¹/2" x width of fabric, binding

INSTRUCTIONS

Design Units

Note: Refer to Strip-Set Panel Nine-Patch Construction, page 13, to make Nine-Patch blocks.

1. Sew a 3¹/2" dusty rose strip to each side of a turquoise strip; cut at 3¹/2" intervals. (**Diagram 1**) Sew a 3¹/2" turquoise strip to each side of a 3¹/2" red strip; cut at 3¹/2" intervals. (**Diagram 2**)

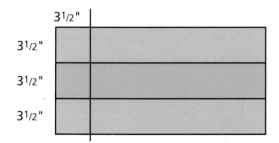

Diagram 1

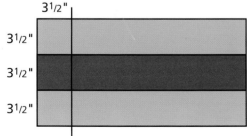

Diagram 2

2. Sew sub-units together to create Nine-Patch block. (**Diagram 3**) Make seven Nine-Patch Starter Blocks.

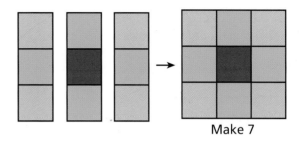

Make 7

Diagram 3

3. Cut each Nine-Patch block into equal quarters. (**Diagram 4**) Measure 1¹/2" from the seam line when cutting. This will make 28 quarters, each measuring 4³/4" x 4³/4".

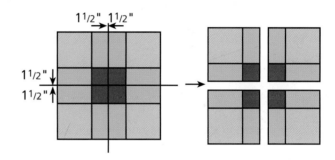

Diagram 4

4. Mark a diagonal pencil line on the wrong side of every quarter-unit. Mark from light corner to light corner. (**Diagram 5**)

Diagram 5

5. Place a marked quarter-unit right sides together with a 4³/4" x 4³/4" terra cotta square over a quarter-unit with right sides together. Using the pencil line as a guide, sew ¹/8" on each side of the line. (**Diagram 6**)

Diagram 6

6. Cut the quarter-unit in half along the diagonal pencil line. Press seam towards the larger triangular piece for design unit A and design unit B. (**Diagram 7**) Repeat with remaining three terra cotta squares and three quarter-units. *Note: You will only use design unit A.*

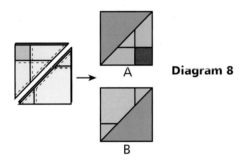

Diagram 7

7. Repeat steps 4 to 6 with remaining quarter-units and sage green squares. (**Diagram 8**) You will use 24 design unit A and 12 design unit B.

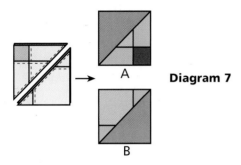

Diagram 8

8. Square by trimming all the design units to 4¹/2" x 4¹/2".

Quilt Assembly
1. Place design units and plain squares in 4 x 6 quarter sections, **Diagram 9**. You will need two of each.

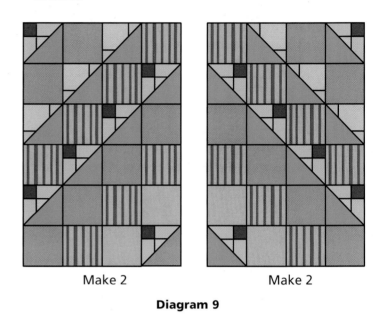

Make 2   Make 2

Diagram 9

2. Join the blocks in each row. Join the rows.

3. Sew two quarter-sections together noting placement; repeat. (**Diagram 10**)

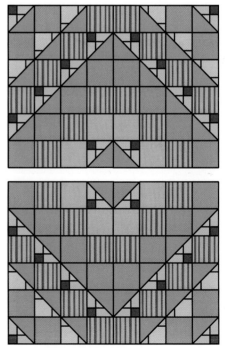

Diagram 10

4. Sew pairs of quarter sections together. (**Diagram 11**)

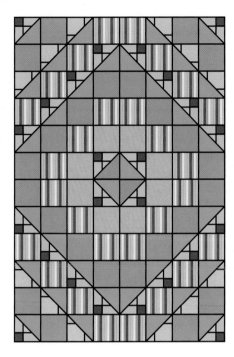

Diagram 11

Note: Refer to Borders with Corner Squares, page 17, to add borders with corners.

5. For first border, sew together 2" red violet strips. Measure across the top and bottom of the quilt and cut two strips to this measurement. Measure length of quilt and cut two strips to this measurement

6. Sew border strips to top and bottom. Sew 2" red squares to each end of remaining borders and sew to sides of quilt.

7. For second border, repeat steps 5 and 6 using 4½" stripe border strips and four design units for the corners.

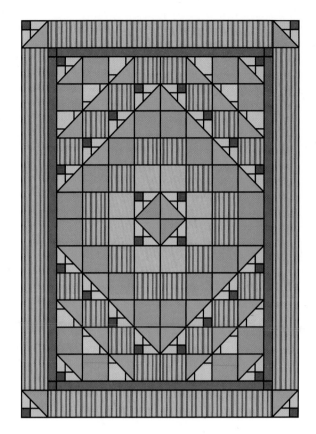

Arizona Road Trip Quilt Layout

8. Layer top, batting and backing and quilt as desired.

9. Make 5½ yards of straight grain binding. See General Directions, page 19, for making and applying binding.

Spring Baskets

*Springtime bursts from this vivid yellow and violet quilt
made mostly from a deep collection of scrap fabrics in those
colors. Some fabric from the border was included in the
body of the quilt for unity.*

Approximate Size: 59" x 89$1/2$"
21 Nine-Patch Starter Blocks: 9" finished
Design Unit Size: 4$3/4$" finished

MATERIALS

Notes: *Fabric requirements are for yellow, light
violet and medium violet fabrics only. If making
a scrap quilt choose fabric equivalent to the
amounts given below. Read ahead to the
measurements given under Cutting.*

*Fabric quantities specified are for 42"/44"-wide,
100% cotton fabrics. All measurements include a
$1/4$-inch seam allowance unless otherwise specified
in the instructions. Sew with right sides together
unless otherwise stated. Press between each sewing
step.*

Nine-Patch Starter Blocks
$5/8$ yard yellow fabric
$5/8$ yard light violet fabric
$1/4$ yard red fabric

Design Units
2$3/4$ yards medium violet fabric

Finishing Triangles and Resting Strips
1 yard light violet fabric

Borders and Binding
$1/2$ yard red fabric
2 yards medium violet fabric

Backing and Batting
5 yards backing fabric
Twin-size batting

CUTTING

Nine-Patch Starter Blocks
8 yellow strips, 3$1/2$" x width of fabric
8 light violet strips, 3$1/2$" x width of fabric
2 red strips, 3$1/2$" x width of fabric

Design Units
84 medium violet squares, 4$3/4$" x 4$3/4$"

Finishing Triangles for Diagonal Set
9 light violet squares, 7$3/4$" x 7$3/4$"
2 light violet squares, 4" x 4"

Borders
6 light violet strips, 1$1/2$" x width of fabric,
    first border (resting strip)
6 strips red, 2" x width of fabric,
    second border
7 strips medium violet, 6" x width of fabric,
    third border

Binding
8 strips medium violet, 2$1/2$" x width of fabric

INSTRUCTIONS

Note: Refer to Strip-Set Panel Nine-Patch Construction, page 13, to make Nine-Patch blocks.

1. Sew a 3½" light violet strip to each side of a 3½" yellow strip. Cut at 3½" intervals. (**Diagram 1**)

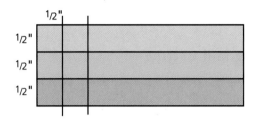

Diagram 1

2. Sew a 3½" yellow strip to each side of a red strip. Cut at 3½" intervals. (**Diagram 2**)

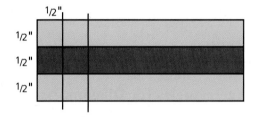

Diagram 2

3. Sew sub-units from steps 1 and 2 together to complete Nine-Patch block. (**Diagram 3**) Make 21 Nine-Patch Starter blocks.

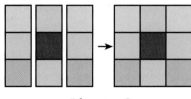

Diagram 3

4. Cut each Nine-Patch block into equal quarters. Measure 1½" from the seam line when cutting. (**Diagram 4**) This will make 84 quarters each measuring 4¾" x 4¾".

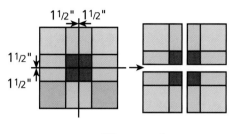

Diagram 4

5. Mark a diagonal pencil line on the wrong side of every quarter-unit. Mark from light corner to light corner. (**Diagram 5**)

 Diagram 5

6. Place a 4¾" medium-violet square right sides together with a quarter-unit. Using the pencil line as a guide, sew ⅛" on each side of the line. (**Diagram 6**)

 Diagram 6

7. Cut the sewn quarter-unit in half along the drawn diagonal line. Press seam towards the larger triangular piece. This step results in two design units – A and B. (**Diagram 7**)

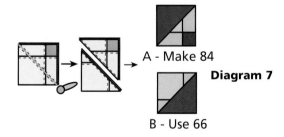

A - Make 84

Diagram 7

B - Use 66

8. Square units by trimming to 4½" x 4½".

60

Quilt Assembly

1. Arrange the A design units into a diagonal quilt set of twelve rows of seven A units. (**Diagram 8**)

2. Fill in the diagonal setting with the B design units and the finishing triangles. (**Diagram 9**)

Diagram 8

Diagram 9

3. Sew quilt together in diagonal rows. (**Diagram 10**) Sew rows together. Add corner triangles last.

Diagram 10

Note: *Refer to Adding Borders, page 16, to add borders.*

4. Measure across the top and bottom of the quilt and cut two 1¹/2" light violet strips to these measurements. Join to the top and bottom of the quilt.

5. Measure length of the quilt and cut two 1¹/2" light violet strips to these measurements. Join to the sides of the quilt.

6. Repeat steps 3 and 4 to add the 2" red and 6" medium violet borders.

7. Layer top, batting and backing and quilt as desired.

8. Make 8 yards of straight grain binding. See General Directions, page 19, for making and applying binding.

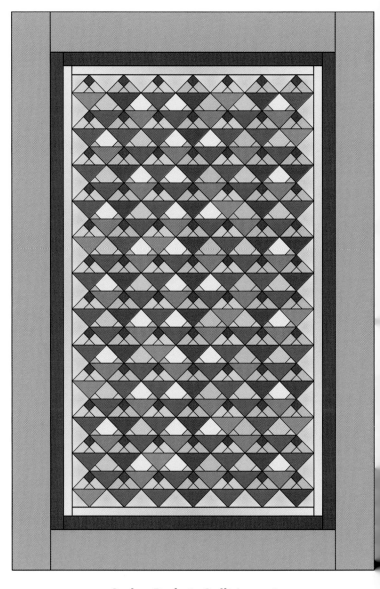

Spring Baskets Quilt Layout

Watermelon Baskets

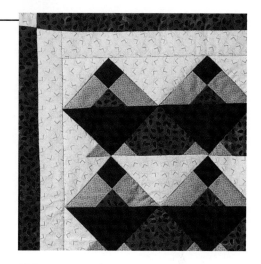

This little quilt will go together quickly – if you pay attention to the details. It is an easy quilt to make, but it is the most challenging quilt in the book.

Approximate Size: 32" x 32"
Three Starter Blocks: 9" finished
Design Unit Size: 4" finished

MATERIALS

Note: Fabric quantities specified are for 42"/44"- wide, 100% cotton fabrics. All measurements include a 1/4-inch seam allowance unless other- wise specified in the instructions. Sew with right sides together unless otherwise stated. Press between each sewing step.

Blocks, Borders, and Binding

1/8 yard dark green
1/4 yard bright green for background
1/4 yard red
1/4 yard black

Batting and Backing

1 yard backing fabric
1 yard batting

CUTTING

Note: To make best use of your fabrics cut in the order given.

Border

4 black strips, 4 1/2" x width of fabric

Starter Blocks

3 black squares, 3 1/2" x 3 1/2"
12 red squares, 3 1/2" x 3 1/2"
12 dark green squares, 3 1/2" x 3 1/2"

Design Units

5 black squares, 4 3/4" x 4 3/4"
   Cut these squares in half on the diagonal.
2 bright green squares, 4 3/4" x 4 3/4"
   Cut these squares in half on the diagonal.

Resting Strips, Setting Pieces, Border and Binding

3 bright green Template A
3 bright green Template A, reversed
6 dark green Template B
6 dark green Template C
2 bright green Template D
1 bright green square, 3 3/4" x 3 3/4"
   Cut square in half on the diagonal.
4 bright green strips, 2" x 20"
   (trim to fit if necessary), first border
4 red strips, 1 3/4" x 22"
   (trim to fit if necessary), second border
4 bright green squares, 1 3/4" x 1 3/4",
   second border corners
4 black border strips, 4 1/2" x 24"
   (trim to fit if necessary), third border
4 bright green squares, 4 1/2" x 4 1/2",
   third border corners
3 black strips, 2 1/2" x width of fabric, binding

INSTRUCTIONS

Making the Blocks

Note: Refer to Traditional Piece-by-Piece Nine-Patch Construction, page 13, to make Nine-Patch blocks.

1. Sew a 3½" red square to opposite sides of a 3½" dark green square; repeat. Sew a 3½" dark green square to opposite sides of a 3½" black square. Sew tows together to make Nine-Patch block. (**Diagram 1**) Make three Nine-Patch blocks.

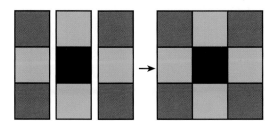

Diagram 1

2. Cut each Nine-Patch block into equal quarters. Measure 1½" from the seam line when cutting. (**Diagram 2**)

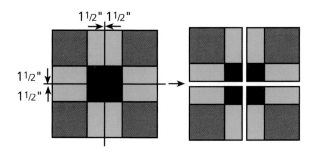

Diagram 2

3. Square the quarter units by trimming to 4¾" x 4¾".

4. Use nine of the quarter units. Mark a diagonal pencil line from green corner to green corner on the **right** side of the unit. (**Diagram 3**)

Diagram 3

5. Place a black triangle right sides together with a quarter-unit. (**Diagram 4**) Next place a bright green triangle right sides together with bottom half of the quarter unit. (**Diagram 5**) Repeat three more times.

Diagram 4

Diagram 5

Note: Place triangles carefully along the pencil line right sides to right sides. Pin in place.

6. Using the pencil line as a presser foot guide sew ⅛" from each side of the drawn line. (**Diagram 6**)

Diagram 6

7. Place a black triangle right sides together with a quarter-unit noting placement; sew ⅛" from drawn line. (**Diagram 7**) Repeat four more times.

Diagram 7

8. Cut all stitched pieces apart on the pencil line. Press the seam toward the large triangle. (**Diagram 8**)

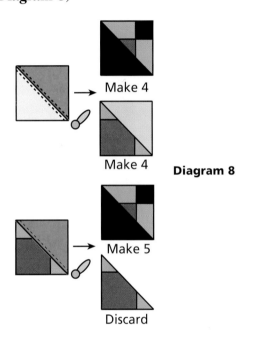

Make 4

Make 4 **Diagram 8**

Make 5

Discard

Quilt Assembly

1. Sew a dark green B triangle to a light green A triangle. Make three of each. (**Diagram 9**)

A
B   B
A   **Diagram 9**

Make 3   Make 3

2. Sew a light green C to A/B triangles. (**Diagram 10**)

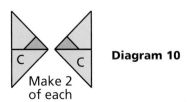

C   C   **Diagram 10**

Make 2
of each

3. Layout the design units and finishing triangles in diagonal rows. (**Diagram 11**); sew the quilt together in diagonal rows. Sew corner triangles to quilt last.

Diagram 11

Note: Refer to Adding Borders, page 16, to add borders.

4. For first border (resting strips), measure across top and bottom of quilt. Cut 2" bright green strips to this measurement and sew to the top and bottom of the quilt. Measure quilt lengthwise. Cut 2" bright green strips to this measurement and sew to sides of quilt.

5. For second border, measure across top and bottom of the quilt and cut two 1³/4" red border strips to this measurement. Measure length of the quilt and cut two 1³/4" red strips to this measurement.

6. Sew strips to top and bottom of quilt. Sew 1³/4" bright green squares to the ends of two remaining 1³/4" red strips. Sew to the sides of the quilt.

7. For third border, repeat steps 5 and 6 using 4½" black strips and 4½" green squares. (**Diagram 12**)

Diagram 12

Watermelon Basket Quilt Layout

8. Layer top, batting and backing and quilt as desired.

9. Make 4 yards of straight grain binding. See General Directions, page 19, for making and applying binding.

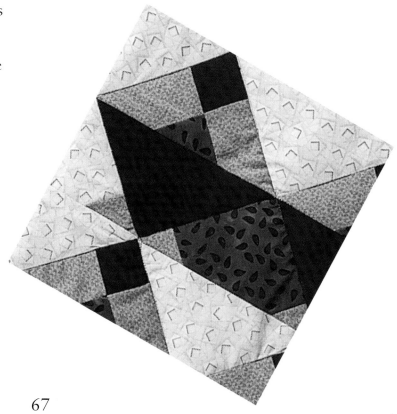

Autumn Stars

Twelve Nine-patch Starter blocks are sliced and diced to construct the twenty-four Master Blocks that make this bold setting. A pieced border creates the outside star points.

Approximate Size: 65$\frac{1}{2}$" x 85$\frac{1}{2}$"

Twelve Nine-Patch Starter Blocks:
   12" finished

Design Unit Size: 5$\frac{1}{4}$" finished

Master Block Size: 10$\frac{1}{2}$" finished

MATERIALS

Note: Fabric quantities specified are for 42"/44"-wide, 100% cotton fabrics. All measurements include a $\frac{1}{4}$-inch seam allowance unless otherwise specified in the instructions. Sew with right sides together unless otherwise stated. Press between each sewing step.

Blocks
   1$\frac{3}{4}$ yards printed muslin
   $\frac{1}{2}$ yard red fabric
   1$\frac{3}{4}$ yards tan fabric
   $\frac{7}{8}$ yard orange fabric
   $\frac{7}{8}$ yard black print fabric

Pieced Border
   $\frac{1}{2}$ yard black print fabric
   1$\frac{1}{4}$ yards orange fabric

Borders and Binding
   1$\frac{1}{2}$ yards black print fabric

Backing and Batting
   5 yards backing fabric
   Full-size batting

Note: Fabric requirements are for five fabrics. If making a scrap quilt, choose fabric equivalent to the amounts given below.

CUTTING

Nine-Patch Starter Blocks
   11 printed muslin strips, 4$\frac{1}{2}$" x width of fabric
   3 red strips, 4$\frac{1}{2}$" x width of fabric
   11 tan strips, 4$\frac{1}{2}$" x width of fabric

Design Units
   24 black print squares, 6$\frac{1}{4}$" x 6$\frac{1}{4}$"
   24 orange squares, 6$\frac{1}{4}$" x 6$\frac{1}{4}$"

Pieced Border
   24 orange squares, 5$\frac{3}{4}$" x 5$\frac{3}{4}$"
   10 black print squares, 6$\frac{1}{8}$" x 6$\frac{1}{8}$"
      Cut each square in half on the diagonal.
   3 orange squares, 11" x 11"
      Cut each in quarters on the diagonal.

Border and Binding
   7 black print strips, 6$\frac{1}{2}$" x width of fabric, border
   8 black print strips, 2$\frac{1}{2}$" x width of fabric, binding

INSTRUCTIONS

Master Block

Note: *Refer to Strip-Set Panel Nine-Patch Construction, page 13, to make Nine-Patch Blocks.*

1. Sew a 4½" printed muslin strip to each side of a 4½" tan strip; cut at 4½" intervals. (**Diagram 1**) Sew a 4½" tan strip to each side of 4½" red strip; cut at 4½" intervals. (**Diagram 2**)

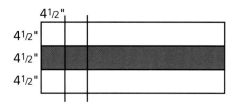

Diagram 1

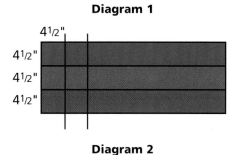

Diagram 2

2. Sew together sub-units from step 1 to create Nine-Patch block. (**Diagram 3**) Make seven Nine-Patch Starter blocks.

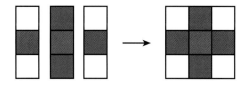

Diagram 3

3. Cut each of the Nine-Patch blocks into equal quarters. Measure 2" from the seam line when cutting. This will make 48 quarters each measuring 6¼" x 6¼". (**Diagram 4**)

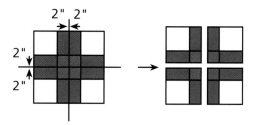

Diagram 4

4. Mark a diagonal pencil line on the wrong side of every quarter-unit. Mark from light corner to light corner. (**Diagram 5**)

Diagram 5

5. Place a 6¼" x 6¼" orange square right sides together with a quarter-unit. Using the pencil line as a guide, sew ⅛" on each side of the drawn line. (**Diagram 1**) Repeat with 23 more quarter-units and orange squares.

Diagram 6

6. Cut the quarter-unit in half along the diagonal pencil line. Press the small seam towards the larger triangular piece. You will have a pair of sub-unit squares from each quarter-unit, sub-unit A and sub-unit B. (**Diagram 7**)

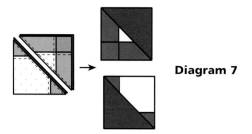

Diagram 7

7. Repeat steps 3 to 6 to sew 24 quarter-units with black squares. (**Diagram 8**)

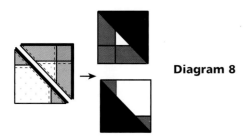

Diagram 8

8. Square design units by trimming to 5¾" x 5¾".

9. Pick up one sub-unit pair with black triangles and one sub-unit pair with orange triangles. Arrange them into a Master Block. Sew the sub-units together in pairs, and then sew pairs together. (**Diagram 9**) Make 24 Master Blocks

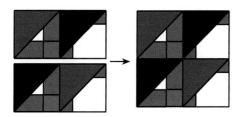

Diagram 9

Quilt Assembly

1. Sew a pair of Master Blocks together; sew pairs together. (**Diagram 10**) Repeat five more times.

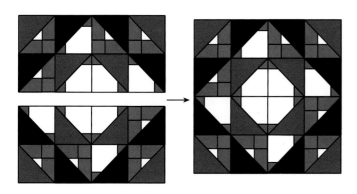

Diagram 10

2. Sew pairs of pairs together in rows, then sew rows together. (**Diagram 11**)

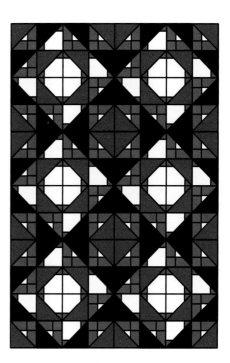

Diagram 11

Note: Refer to Adding Borders, page 16, to add borders.

3. For the first (pieced) border, sew black print triangles to adjacent sides of large orange triangles. (**Diagram 12**) Make ten Flying Geese units.

Diagram 12

4. Sew a 5¾" orange square to each side of Flying Geese unit (**Diagram 13**)

Diagram 13

5. Sew two units from step 2 together; repeat. Sew to top and bottom of quilt.

6. Sew three units from step 2 together. Sew an orange square to each end; repeat. Sew to sides of quilt. (**Diagram 14**)

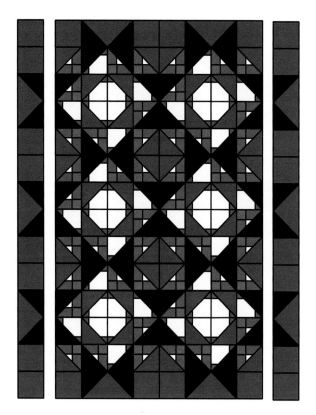

Diagram 14

Auumn Stars Quilt Layout

7. For second border, measure quilt across top and bottom; cut two 6½" black strips to that length and sew to top and bottom. Measure quilt length. Cut two 6½" black strips to that length and sew to sides of quilt.

8. Layer top, batting and backing and quilt as desired.

9. Make 8½ yards of straight grain binding. See General Directions, page 19, for making and applying binding.

Small Medallion

Make only two Nine-Patch Blocks to create this stunning *Small Medallion* quilt! The graphic prints, as well as, hand-dyed and marbleized fabrics, add to the excitement.

Approximate Size: 28" x 28"
Two Nine-Patch Starter Blocks: 9" finished
Design Unit Size: 4¹/4" x 4¹/4" finished

MATERIALS

Note: Fabric quantities specified are for 42"/44"-wide, 100% cotton fabrics. All measurements include a ¹/4-inch seam allowance unless otherwise specified in the instructions. Sew with right sides together unless otherwise stated. Press between each sewing step.

Fat quarter black fabric
Fat quarter marbleized fabric
Scrap red violet fabric
Scrap turquoise fabric
Fat quarter graphic print
¹/8 yard check fabric
³/4 hand-painted fabric
1 yard backing fabric
Batting

CUTTING

Two Starter Blocks

8 black squares, 3¹/2" x 3¹/2"
8 marbleized fabric squares, 3¹/2" x 3¹/2"
1 red violet square, 3¹/2" x 3¹/2"
1 turquoise squares, 3¹/2" x 3¹/2"

Design Units

4 graphic print squares, 4³/4" x 4³/4"
4 hand-painted squares, 4³/4" x 4³/4"

Borders

2 check fabric strips, 1¹/2" x width
2 hand-painted fabric strips, 5¹/2" x width, border
3 hand-painted strips, 2¹/2" x width, binding

INSTRUCTIONS

Note: *Refer to Traditional Piece-by-piece Nine-Patch Construction, page 13, to make Nine-Patch blocks.*

1. Sew 3½" marbleized print square to opposite sides of a 3½" black square; repeat. Sew 3½" black square to opposite sides of 3½" red violet red square. Sew rows together to complete Nine Patch A block (**Diagram 1**)

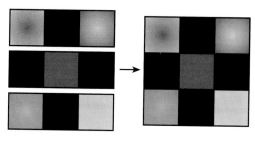

Diagram 1

2. Repeat step 1 substituting a 3½" turquoise square for the red violet square to complete Nine-Patch B block. (**Diagram 2**)

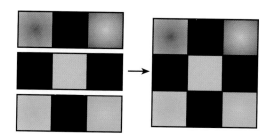

Diagram 2

3. Cut each Nine-Patch block into equal quarters. Measure 1½" from the seam line when cutting. This will make eight quarters each measuring 4¾" x 4¾". (**Diagram 3**)

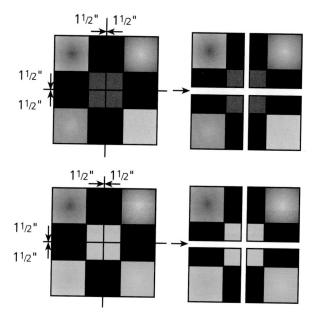

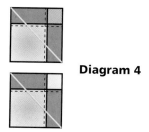

Diagram 3

4. Mark a diagonal white pencil line on the wrong side of every quarter-unit. Mark from black corner to black corner. (**Diagram 4**)

Diagram 4

5. Place a 4¾" graphic print square right sides together with a quarter-unit from Nine-Patch A. Using the pencil line as a guide sew ⅛" on each side of the line. (**Diagram 5**)

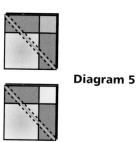

Diagram 5

77

Blue Medallion

Four Nine-Patch Starter Blocks are needed for this eye-catching Blue Medallion quilt. Predominant use of blue scrap fabrics and the bold batik unify the quilt.

Approximate Size: 35$^{1}/2$" x 35$^{1}/2$"
Four Nine-Patch Starter Blocks: 9" finished
Design Unit Size: 4" finished

MATERIALS

Starter Blocks, Design Units, Border
$^{2}/3$ yard batik fabric
   (starter blocks, design units, border)
$^{1}/4$ yard blue print fabric
Assorted fabric scraps
   (large enough for 3$^{1}/2$" squares)
10" square black fabric

Binding
$^{1}/3$ yard blue stripe fabric

Backing and Batting
1$^{1}/8$ yards backing fabric
1$^{1}/8$ yds batting

CUTTING

Note: *Fabric quantities specified are for 42"/44"-wide, 100% cotton fabrics. All measurements include a ? inch seam allowance unless otherwise specified in the instructions. Sew with right sides together unless otherwise stated. Press between each sewing step.*

Starter Blocks
4 black squares, 3$^{1}/2$" x 3$^{1}/2$"
16 scrap fabric squares, 3$^{1}/2$" x 3$^{1}/2$"
16 muslin squares, 3$^{1}/2$" x 3$^{1}/2$"

Design Units
16 assorted batik and blue squares,
   4$^{3}/4$" x 4$^{3}/4$"

Borders
4 blue rectangles, 4$^{1}/2$" x 8$^{1}/2$"
4 batik strips, 5$^{3}/4$" x width of fabric

Binding
4 blue stripe strips, 2$^{1}/2$" x width of fabric

INSTRUCTIONS

Design Units
Note: *Refer to Traditional Piece-by-Piece Nine-Patch Construction, page 13, to make Nine-Patch blocks,*

1. Sew a 3$^{1}/2$" square to opposite sides of a 3$^{1}/2$" muslin square; repeat. Sew a 3$^{1}/2$" muslin square to opposite sides of a 3$^{1}/2$" black square. Sew rows together to complete Nine-Patch block. (**Diagram 1**) Make four Nine-Patch Starter Blocks.

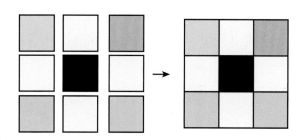

81

Diagram 1

2. Cut each of the Nine-Patch blocks into equal quarters. Measure 1¹/2" from the seam line when cutting. This will make 16 quarters each measuring 4³/4" x 4³/4". (**Diagram 2**)

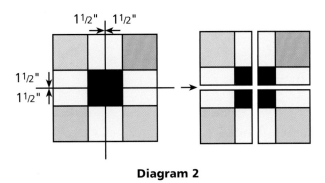

Diagram 2

3. Mark a diagonal pencil line on the wrong side of every quarter-unit. Mark from light corner to light corner. (**Diagram 3**)

Diagram 3

4. Place a 4³/4" x 4³/4" blue or batik square right sides together with marked quarter-unit. Using the pencil line as a guide sew ¹/8" on each side of the line. (**Diagram 4**)

Diagram 4

5. Cut the quarter-unit in half along the diagonal pencil line. Press seam towards the larger triangular piece. This step results in two design units – A and B. (**Diagram 5**)

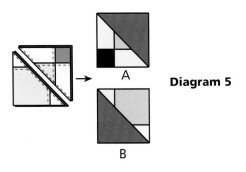

Diagram 5

6. Square design units by trimming to 4¹/2 " x 4¹/2".

Quilt Assembly

1. Arrange four design units into pairs. Sew in rows, then sew rows together. (**Diagram 6**) Make three more quarter sections.

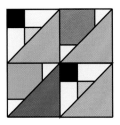

Make 4

Diagram 6

2. Sew two quarters together noting positions; repeat. Sew pairs of quarter sections together. (**Diagram 7**)

Diagram 7

Note: *Refer to Adding Borders, page 16, to add borders.*

3. Sew a B design unit to each of end of four blue border rectangles. (**Diagram 8**) Add an A design unit to each end of two of the borders for the sides. (**Diagram 9**) *Note: There will be four A units left over.*

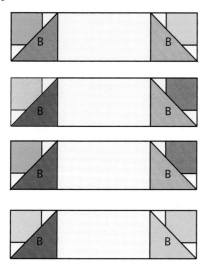

Diagram 8

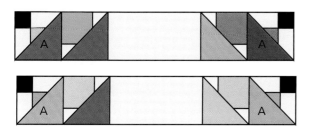

Diagram 9

4. Sew the pieced border to the top and bottom first, then to the sides. (**Diagram 10**)

Diagram 10

5. For the second border, measure across the top and bottom of the quilt and cut two batik strips to these measurements. Sew to top and bottom of quilt. Measure sides of the quilt and cut two batik strips to these measurements. Sew to the sides.

6. Layer top, batting and backing and quilt as desired.

7. Make 4 yards of straight grain binding. See General Directions, page 19, for making and applying binding.

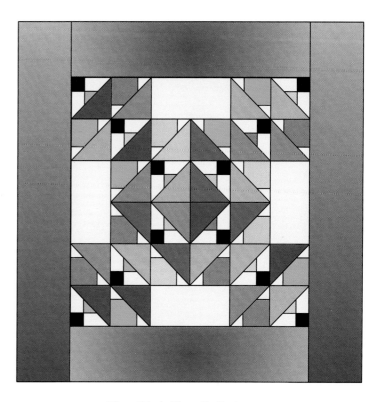

Blue Medallion Quilt Layout

83

Dragonfly

The scrap fabrics in the Dragonfly Quilt emulate the appearance of those found in a nineteenth century quilt. The fabrics are modern and most are not replicas, but they reflect those fabrics available from about 1860 to 1910. The Dragonfly Block is unique to the Disappearing Nine-Patch technique.

Approximate Size: 74" x 98"
18 Nine-Patch Starter Blocks: 9" finished
Dragonfly Block Size: 10" square finished

MATERIALS

Notes: *Fabric requirements are for light, medium and dark fabrics only. If making a scrap quilt choose fabric equivalent to the amounts given below. Read ahead to the measurements given under Cutting.*

Fabric quantities specified are for 42"/44"-wide, 100% cotton fabrics. All measurements include a $1/4$-inch seam allowance unless otherwise specified in the instructions. Sew with right sides together unless otherwise stated. Press each seam after sewing.

Nine-Patch Starter Blocks
$1/2$ yard dark or medium dark fabric
$1 1/2$ yards light fabric
$1 1/2$ yards medium fabric

To finish Dragonfly Block Units
1 yard light medium to medium fabric
1 yard medium dark fabric

Sashing and Hourglass Cornerstones
$5/8$ yard strawberry pink fabric
$5/8$ yard white fabric
$1 1/2$ yards green fabric

Borders and Binding
$2/3$ yard strawberry pink fabric
$1 1/2$ yards green fabric

Batting and Backing
6 yards backing
Queen-size batting

CUTTING

Starter Nine-Patch Blocks
18 dark fabric squares, $3 1/2$" x $3 1/2$"
72 light and medium fabric squares total, $4 1/2$" x $4 1/2$"
72 medium fabric rectangles, $3 1/2$" x $4 1/2$"

Dragonfly Blocks
70 medium or medium-dark fabric squares, $5 3/4$" x $5 3/4$"

Note: *If using scraps each finished block requires two squares of the same fabric.*

Sashing and Hourglass Cornerstones
82 green rectangles, $2 1/2$" x $10 1/2$", sashing
48 white and 48 pink squares, $3 1/4$" x $3 1/4$", Hourglass Cornerstones

Borders
8 strawberry pink strips, $2 1/2$" x width of fabric
4 light fabric squares, $2 1/2$" x $2 1/2$"
8 green strips, $4 1/2$" x width of border
4 strawberry pink squares, $4 1/2$" x $4 1/2$"

Binding
9 green strips, $2 1/2$" x width of fabric

INSTRUCTIONS

Dragonfly Blocks

Note: *Refer to the Traditional Piece-by-Piece Nine-Patch Construction, page 13, to make Nine-Patch blocks. This quilt requires one type of Starter Block with colors and values arranged in different ways.*

1. Sew a 4¹/2" light or medium square to each side of a 3¹/2" x 4¹/2" medium rectangle; repeat. Sew a 3¹/2" x 4¹/2" medium rectangle to each side of a 3¹/2" dark square. Sew rows together for Nine-Patch block. (**Diagram 1**) Make 18 Nine-Patch Starter blocks.

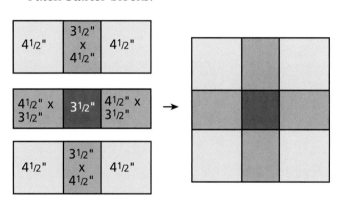

Diagram 1

2. Quarter cut all 18 blocks by measuring 1¹/2" from seam. (**Diagram 2**) This will make 72 quarters each measuring 5³/4" x 5³/4". Trim to this size if necessary.

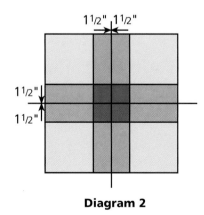

Diagram 2

3. Mark a diagonal pencil line on the wrong side of every quarter-unit. (**Diagram 3**)

Diagram 3

4. Place a 5³/4" x 5³/4" print square right side together with a quarter-unit. Using the pencil line as a guide, sew either ¹/8" or ¹/4" on either side of the line. (**Diagram 4**)

Diagram 4

Note: *Using a ¹/8" seam allowance, in this instance, will result in a finished 10" Dragonfly Block.*

5. Cut the quarter-unit in half along the diagonal pencil line. Press seam towards the larger triangular piece. This step will result in two design units – A and B. (**Diagram 5**)

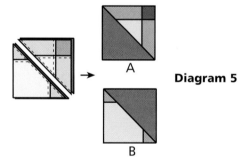

Diagram 5

6. Square each design unit to 5¹/2".

7. Sew an A and B design unit together; repeat. Sew pairs together to complete a Dragonfly block. (**Diagram 6**) Make 35 blocks. Square each block to 10½".

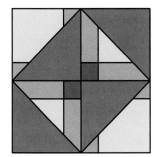

Make 35 Dragonfly Blocks

Diagram 6

Sashing & Hour Glass Cornerstones

Note: The formula for creating a quick pieced Hourglass Block is: add 1¼" to the finished "Hourglass" measurement. For a traditional 19th Century Dragonfly quilt, the starting squares should be strawberry pink and white and cut 3¼" x 3¼".

1. Draw a diagonal line from corner to corner on each 3¼" white square. Place marked white square right sides together with 3¼" strawberry pink square. Stitch ¼" from each side of the diagonal line. (**Diagram 7**)

Diagram 7

2. Cut the squares in half along the drawn diagonal line. Press the seams open. (**Diagram 8**)

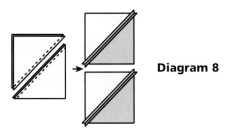

Diagram 8

3. On the wrong side of one triangle square draw a diagonal line from corner to corner through each color triangle. (**Diagram 9**) Repeat this step on half the triangle square units.

Diagram 9

4. Place a marked triangle square right sides together with a second unmarked triangle square. (**Diagram 10**) *Note: Contrasting fabrics should face each other. Lift a corner to make sure they are in the correct position. Pin at center for accuracy.*

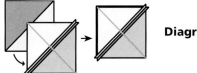

Diagram 10

5. Stitch ¼" from each side of the drawn diagonal line. (**Diagram 11**)

Diagram 11

6. Cut the squares in half on the diagonal line. Press seams open. (**Diagram 12**)

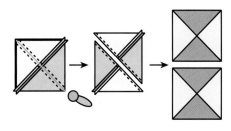

Diagram 12

Quilt Assembly

1. Assemble the quilt in rows. Sew six 2½" x 10½" green sashing strips alternately with five Dragonfly blocks; make seven block rows. Sew six Hourglass Cornerstones alternately with five 2½" x 10½" green sashing strips; make eight sashing rows. (**Diagram 13**)

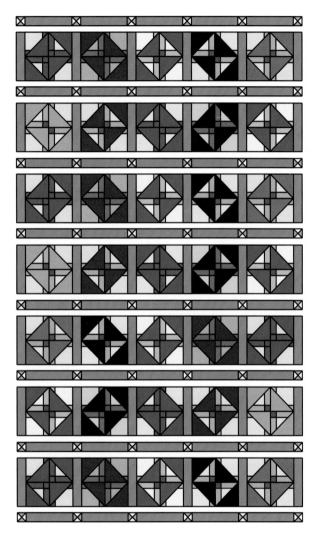

Diagram 13

2. Sew the rows together.

Note: *Refer to Borders with Corner Squares, page 17, to add borders with corners.*

3. For first border, measure across the top and bottom of the quilt and cut two 2½" strawberry pink fabric strips to this measurement. Next, measure the sides and cut two 2½" strawberry pink fabric strips to this measurement. Sew border strips to the top and bottom of the quilt. Sew the white squares to the ends of remaining strips and join to the sides of the quilt body.

4. Repeat step 3 with 4½" green strips and 4½" pink squares.

5. Layer top, batting and backing and quilt as desired.

6. Make 9 yards of straight grain binding. See General Directions, page 19, for making and applying binding.

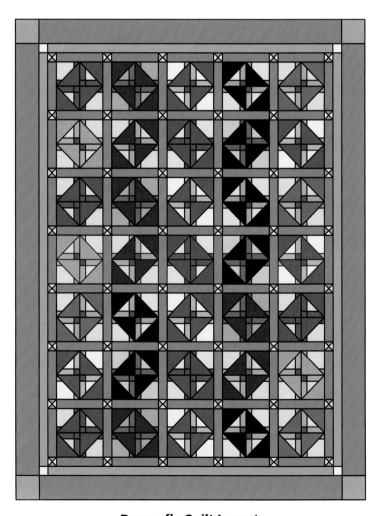

Dragonfly Quilt Layout

OTHER SIZES

	Baby/ Small Lap	Full/Queen	King
Size without Border	38" x 50"	86" x 98"	98" x 98"
Size with Border	51" x 63"	99" x 111"	111" x 111"
Starter Blocks	8	28	32
DragonFly Blocks 10"	15	56	64

Yardage

Starter Blocks

Dark	1/4 yard	3/4 yard	1 yard
Light	3/4 yard	2 yards	2 1/2 yards
Medium	3/4 yard	2 yards	2 1/2 yards

To Finish DragonFly Blocks

Light Medium	1/2 yard	7/8 yard	1 yard
Medium Dark	1/2 yard	7/8 yard	1 yard
Cornerstones **Pink** **White**	 3/8 yard 3/8 yard	 3/4 yard 3/4 yard	 7/8 yard 7/8 yard
Sashing	7/8 yard	2 yards	2 1/4 yards
Border	7/8 yard	1 1/2 yards	1 5/8 yards
Binding	1/2 yard	1 yard	1 yard

Blue OP

This setting and selection of fabrics is a grand way to use up a really odd-lot collection of same color and similar value fabrics. The very strong grid produced by the black and white fabrics will cause almost any color combination to retreat into the background. In this quilt, the black in the grid creates mild optical illusion by often disappearing into the blue fabrics.

Approximate Size: 93¹/₂" x 93¹/₂"
Nine-Patch Starter Blocks: 50 Block A and 50 Block B, 9" finished
Finished Block Size: 8¹/₂" square

MATERIALS

Note: Fabric quantities specified are for 42"/44"-wide, 100% cotton fabrics. All measurements include a ¹/₄-inch seam allowance unless otherwise specified in the instructions. Sew with right sides together unless otherwise stated. Press each seam after sewing.

Blocks
4 yards assorted medium blue fabrics
2¹/₂ yards black fabric
2¹/₂ yards white fabric

Border and Binding
2¹/₂ yards assorted blue fabrics

Backing and Batting
7¹/₂ yards backing fabric
King-size batting

CUTTING

Note: To make best use of your fabrics cut in the order given.

Blocks
34 assorted blue strips, 3¹/₂" x width of fabric
21 black strips, 3¹/₂" x width of fabric
21 white strips, 3¹/₂" x width of fabric

Border
84 blue squares, 4³/₄" x 4³/₄", border

Binding
9 blue strips, 2¹/₂" x width of fabric, binding

INSTRUCTIONS

The Starter Blocks
Note: Refer to Strip-Set Panel Construction, page 13, to make Nine-Patch blocks.

1. Sew a 3¹/₂" blue strip to each side of a 3¹/₂" black strip. Cut strip set at 3¹/₂" intervals. (**Diagram 1**) Sew a 3¹/₂" black strip to each side of a 3¹/₂" white strip. Cut strip set at 3¹/₂" intervals. (**Diagram 2**)

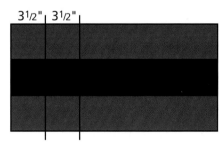

3¹/₂" 3¹/₂"

Diagram 1

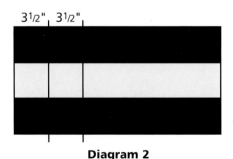

3¹/₂" 3¹/₂"

Diagram 2

91

2. Sew sub-units together to form Nine-Patch Block A. (**Diagram 3**) Make 50 Nine-Patch A.

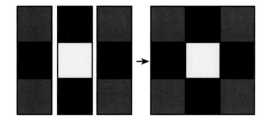

Diagram 3

3. Sew a 3¹/₂" blue strip to each side of a 3¹/₂" white strip. Cut strip set at 3¹/₂" intervals. (**Diagram 4**) Sew a 3¹/₂" white strip to each side of a 3¹/₂" black strip. Cut strip set at 3¹/₂" intervals. (**Diagram 5**)

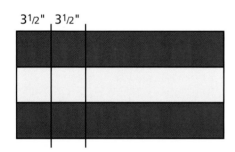

Diagram 4

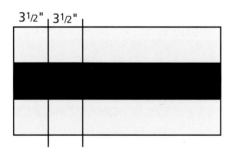

Diagram 5

4. Sew sub-units together to form Nine-Patch Block B, **Diagram 6.** Make 50 Nine-Patch B.

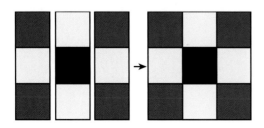

Diagram 6

5. Quarter cut all 100 blocks by measuring 1¹/₂" from inside seams. Make a vertical and a horizontal cut. (**Diagram 7**)

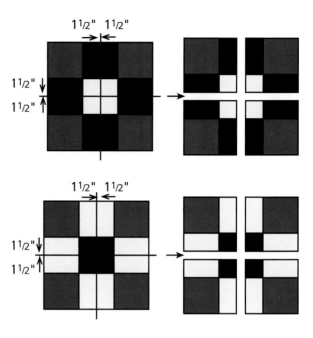

Diagram 7

6. Sew a design unit from Nine-Patch A to one from Nine-Patch B; repeat. Sew pairs together to complete block. (**Diagram 8**) Make 100 Nine-Patch Blue Op blocks.

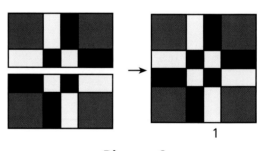

Diagram 8

7. Square by trimming the blocks to 9".

Quilt Assembly

Hint: This quilt design lends itself to being assembled in quarters, including the border application. It is easier to assemble and to machine quilt.

1. Lay out each quarter into five rows of five blocks. Join the blocks in each row and then join the rows. (**Diagram 9**)

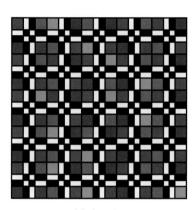

Make 4

Diagram 9

2. For pieced border, sew together ten 4³/4" blue squares into a long border strip. Make three more border strips in the same manner.

3. Sew pieced strip to tops of each quarter section. (**Diagram 10**)

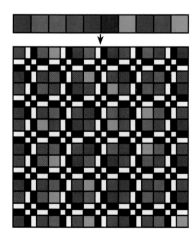

Diagram 10

4. Sew together eleven 4³/4" blue squares into a long border strip. Make three more border strips in the same manner. Sew a pieced strip to the left side of two quarter sections; sew a pieced strip to the right side of the remaining two quarter sections. (**Diagram 11**)

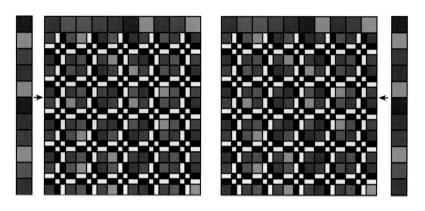

Diagram 11

5. Sew quarter sections together in pairs, then sew pairs together. (**Diagram 12**)

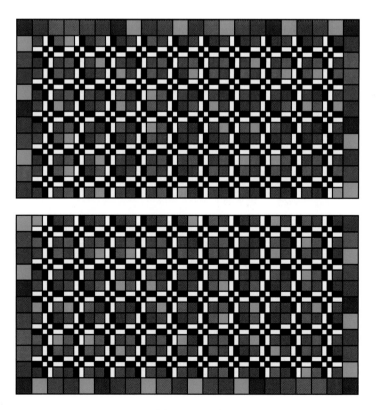

Diagram 12

93

6. Layer top, batting and backing and quilt as desired.

7. Make 11 yards of straight grain binding. See General Directions, page 19, for making and applying binding.

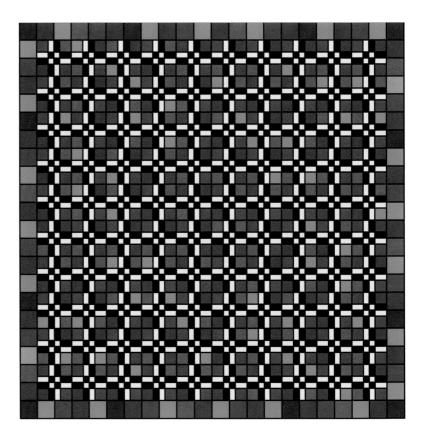

Blue Op Quilt Layout

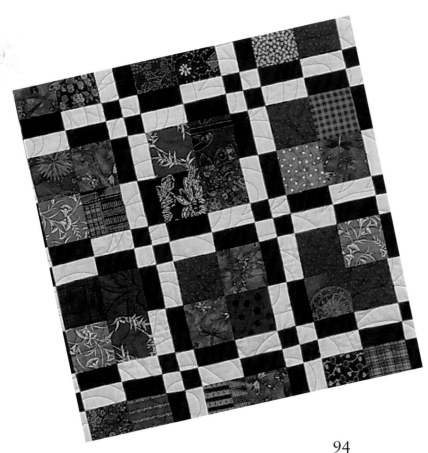

94

OTHER SIZES

	Baby/Small Lap	Twin	Full/Queen	King
Blue Op Blocks	15	88	99	121
Blocks Set	3 x 5	8 x 11	9 x 11	11 x 11
Size (no borders)	25½" x 42¾"	68" x 93½"	76½" x 93½"	93½" x 93½"
Border	36 squares @ 4¾" x 4¾" Adds 8½"	80 squares @ 4¾" x 4¾" Adds 8½"	84 squares @ 4¾" x 4¾" Adds 8½"	92 squares @ 4¾" x 4¾" Adds 8½"
Binding Strips	5 @ 2½" x width	9 @ 2½" x width	10 @ 2½" x width	11 @ 2½" x width
Finished Size	34" x 51"	76½" x 102"	85" x 102"	102" x 102"

Yardage

	Baby/Small Lap	Twin	Full/Queen	King
Assorted Blues	8 strips 3½" x 22"	32 strips 3½" x 44"	40 strips 3½" x 44"	48 Strips 3½" x 44"
White	½ yard	2 yards	2¼ yards	2½ yards
Black	½ yard	2 yards	2¼ yards	2½ yards
Border	¾ yard	1½ yards	1¾ yards	2 yards
Binding	½ yard	¾ yard	¾ yard	⅞ yard

Floating Grid

The design of this quilt suggests the illusion of depth. The construction is easy. Design Units are first sewn into blocks, assembled and then surrounded with a pieced border.

Approximate Size: 39" x 39"

Ten Starter Blocks—five A and five B:
  10" finished

Design Unit Size: 4³/4" finished

MATERIALS

Note: *Fabric quantities specified are for 42"/44"-wide, 100% cotton fabrics. All measurements include a ¹/4-inch seam allowance unless otherwise specified in the instructions. Sew with right sides together unless otherwise stated. Press between each sewing step.*

Blocks, Borders and Binding
  ¹/3 yard batik fabric
  1¹/2 yards total, black and white prints
  ¹/3 yard chrome yellow fabric
  ¹/3 yard violet fabric
  ¹/8 yard black fabric
  ¹/8 yard white fabric

Batting and Backing
  1¹/4 yards backing fabric
  1¹/4 yards batting

CUTTING

Starter Blocks and Pieced Border
  3 batik strips, 4¹/2" x width of fabric
  2 chrome yellow strips, 4¹/2" x width of fabric
  3 black and white strips, 4¹/2" x width of fabric
  2 violet strips, 4¹/2" x width of fabric
  1¹/2 chrome yellow strips, 2¹/2" x width
    of fabric
  1 black strip, 2¹/2" x width of fabric
  1 white strip, 2¹/2" x width of fabric
  1¹/2 violet strips, 2¹/2" x width of fabric
  2 white squares, 1¹/4" x 1¹/4"
  2 black squares, 1¹/4" x 1¹/4"

Border and Binding
  5 black and white print strips, 5" x width
    of fabric
  5 black and white print strips, 2¹/2" x width
    of fabric

INSTRUCTIONS

Making the Blocks

Note: Refer to Strip-Set Panel Nine-Patch Construction, page 13, to make Nine-Patch blocks.

1. Sew a 4¹/2" batik strip to each side of a 2¹/2" chrome yellow strip. Cut strip set at 4¹/2" intervals for a total of ten sub-units. Sew a 4¹/2" chrome yellow strip to each side of a 2¹/2" black strip. Cut strip set at 2¹/2" intervals for a total of five sub-units. (**Diagram 1**)

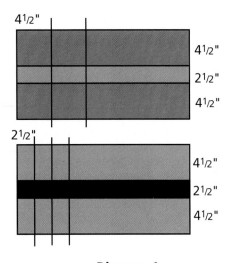

Diagram 1

2. Sew sub-units together to make Nine-Patch A. (**Diagram 2**) Make a total of five Nine-Patch A.

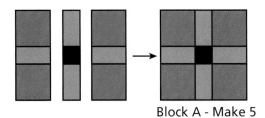

Block A - Make 5

Diagram 2

3. Sew a 4¹/2" black and white strip to each side of a 2¹/2" violet strip. Cut strip set at 4¹/2" intervals for a total of ten sub-units. Sew a 4¹/2" violet strip to each side of a 2¹/2" black and white strip. Cut strip set at 2¹/2" intervals for a total of five sub-units. (**Diagram 3**)

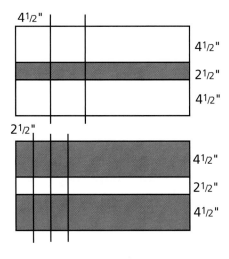

Diagram 3

4. Sew sub-units together to make Nine-Patch B. (**Diagram 4**) Make a total of five Nine-Patch B.

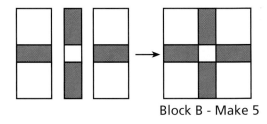

Block B - Make 5

Diagram 4

5. Cut each Nine-Patch block into equal quarters. Measure 1" from the seam line when cutting. (**Diagram 5**)

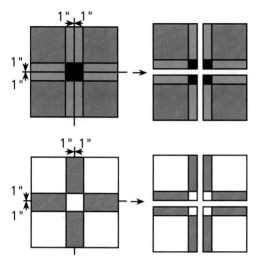

Diagram 5

6. Square the quarter-units by trimming to 5¼" x 5¼" if needed

7. Sew quarter-units into pairs and then sew pairs together to complete block. (**Diagram 6**) Make a total of nine Blocks. Blocks will measure 10" (9½" finished) square. You will have one leftover block.

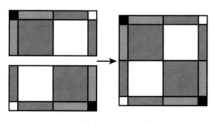

Diagram 6

Quilt Assembly

1. Sew the blocks together in three rows of three blocks each. (**Diagram 7**)

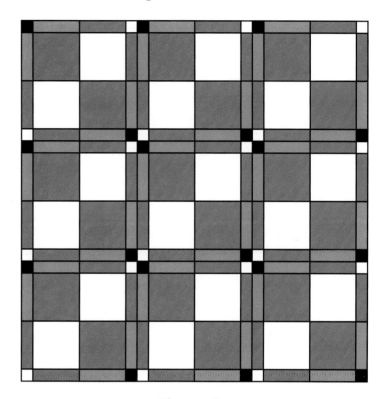

Diagram 7

2. For pieced border, cut three sub-units each from chrome/black and violet/black/white strip sets. (**Diagram 8**)

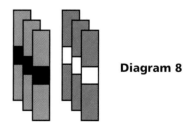

Diagram 8

3. Quarter-cut the sub-units. (**Diagram 9**)

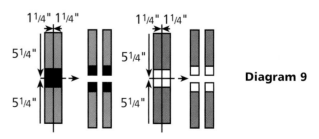

Diagram 9

4. Sew three of each sub-unit together to form a border strip. (**Diagram 10**) Make four border strips.

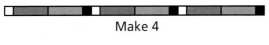

Make 4

Diagram 10

5. Sew a pieced border to top and bottom of quilt body. Sew a 1¼" black square to one end and a 1¼" black and white square to opposite end of remaining borders and sew to sides of quilt. (**Diagram 11**)

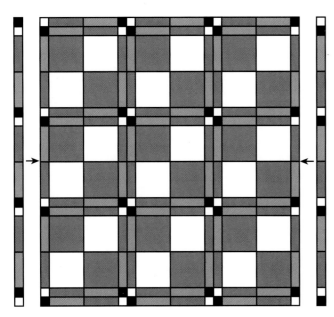

Diagram 11

6. Measure the quilt across top and bottom. Cut 5" black and white strips to that length and sew to top and bottom of quilt. Measure length of quilt. Cut 5" black and white strips to that length and sew to sides of quilt.

7. Layer top, batting and backing and quilt as desired.

8. Make 5 yards of straight grain binding. See General Directions, page 19, for making and applying binding.

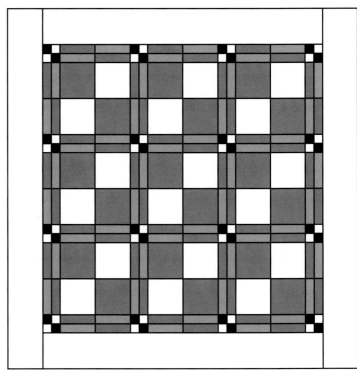

Floating Grid Quilt Layout

Large Blue Star

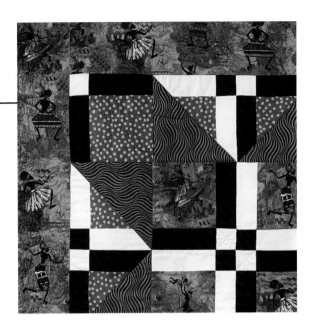

The scale and open areas of the large block is perfect to display a special fabric. There are four types of Starter Nine Patch blocks in this quilt. Make one each.

Approximate Size: 40" x 40"
Four Nine-Patch Starter Blocks:
  15" finished
Design Unit Size: 7" finished
Star Block Size: 28" finished

MATERIALS

Note: Fabric quantities specified are for 42"/44"-wide, 100% cotton fabrics. All measurements include a 1/4-inch seam allowance unless otherwise specified in the instructions. Sew with right sides together unless otherwise stated. Press between each sewing step.

Blocks, Border and Binding
  3/4 yard orange print
  1/2 yard blue fabric
  1/3 yard black fabric
  1/3 yard muslin
  1 yard gold print

Backing and Batting
  1 1/2 yard backing fabric
  1 1/2 yards batting

CUTTING

Nine-Patch Starter Blocks:
  12 orange print squares, 6 " x 6"
  4 gold print squares, 6" x 6"
  2 black squares, 4 1/2" x 4 1/2"
  2 muslin squares, 4 1/2" x 4 1/2"
  8 black rectangles, 4 1/2" x 6"
  8 muslin rectangles, 4 1/2 " x 6"

Design Units
  8 blue squares, 7 3/4" x 7 3/4"

Border
  4 gold print strips, 5 3/4" x width of fabric

Binding
  4 orange print strips 2 1/2" x width of fabric

INSTRUCTIONS

Design Units

Note: Refer to Traditional Piece-by-Piece Nine-Patch Construction, page 13, to make Nine-Patch blocks.

1. Make four Nine-Patch blocks, referring to placement in **Diagram 1.**

2. Cut each Nine-Patch block into equal quarters. Measure 2" from the seam line when cutting. (**Diagram 2**)

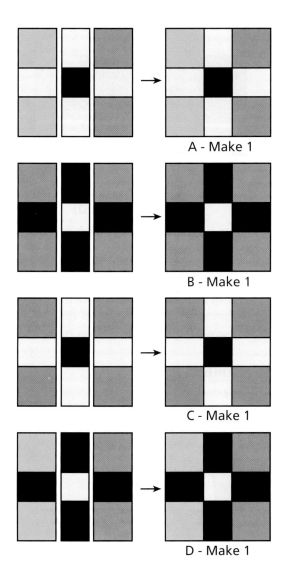

A - Make 1

B - Make 1

C - Make 1

D - Make 1

Diagram 1

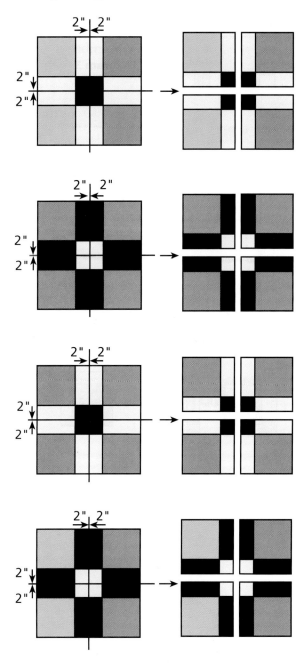

Diagram 2

Tuscan Stars

When I first designed this star block I thought it looked like a fragment of an Italian mosaic floor. There are four types of Starter Nine Patch blocks in this quilt.

Approximate Size: 42" x 42"
17 Nine-Patch Starter Blocks: 9" finished
Design Unit Size: 4" finished
Tuscan Star Block: 17" finished

MATERIALS

Note: Fabric quantities specified are for 42"/44"-wide, 100% cotton fabrics. All measurements include a 1/4-inch seam allowance unless otherwise specified in the instructions. Sew with right sides together unless otherwise stated. Press between each sewing step.

Blocks, Border and Binding
1 1/3 yards light background print (includes border and binding)
1/3 yard blue fabric
1/3 yard tan fabric
1/8 yard gold print
1/8 yard green print
3/4 yard red print

Backing and Batting
1 1/2 yards backing fabric
1 1/2 yards batting

CUTTING

Nine-Patch Starter Blocks
4 light background strips, 3 1/2 " x width of fabric
4 blue strips, 3 1/2" x width of fabric
4 tan strips, 3 1/2" x width of fabric
3 gold strips, 3 1/2 " x width of fabric
1 green strip, 3 1/2" x width of fabric
5 strips red, 4 3/4" x width of fabric
   Cut the red strips into squares, 4 3/4" x 4 3/4"

Border
4 strips light, 4 3/4" x width of fabric

Binding
5 strips 2 1/2" x width of fabric

INSTRUCTIONS

Tuscan Star Block

Note: Refer to Strip-Set Panel Nine-Patch Construction, page 13, to make Nine-Patch blocks. Pay close attention to the fabric placement and the number of each type of block required for this quilt.

1. For Nine-Patch A, sew a 3½" light background strip to each side of a 3½" blue strip. Sew 3½" blue strip to each side of a 3½" tan strip. Cut strip sets in 3½" intervals. (**Diagram 1**) Sew sub-units together to make Nine-Patch A block. (**Diagram 2**) Make six blocks.

2. For Nine-Patch B, sew a 3½" light background strip to each side of a 3½" gold strip. Sew 3½" gold strip to each side of a 3½" green strip. Cut strip sets in 3½" intervals. (**Diagram 3**) Sew sub-units together to make Nine-Patch B block. (**Diagram 4**) Make six blocks.

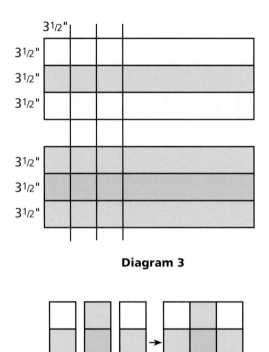

Diagram 3

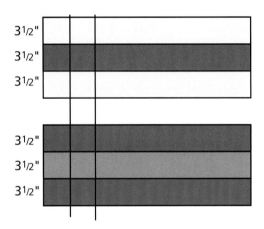

Diagram 1

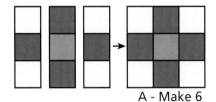

A - Make 6

Diagram 2

Diagram 4

3. For Nine-Patch C, sew a 3¹/2" tan strip to each side of a 3¹/2" blue strip. Sew 3¹/2" blue strip to each side of a 3¹/2" tan strip. Cut strip sets in 3¹/2" intervals. (**Diagram 5**) Sew sub-units together to make Nine-Patch C block. (**Diagram 6**) Make three blocks.

4. For Nine-Patch D, sew a 3¹/2" tan strip to each side of a 3¹/2" gold strip. Sew 3¹/2" gold strip to each side of a 3¹/2" green strip. Cut strip sets in 3¹/2" intervals. (**Diagram 7**) Sew sub-units together to make Nine-Patch D block. (**Diagram 8**) Make two blocks.

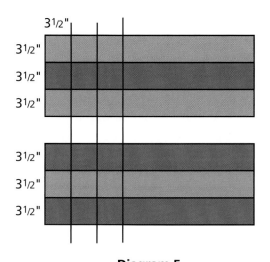

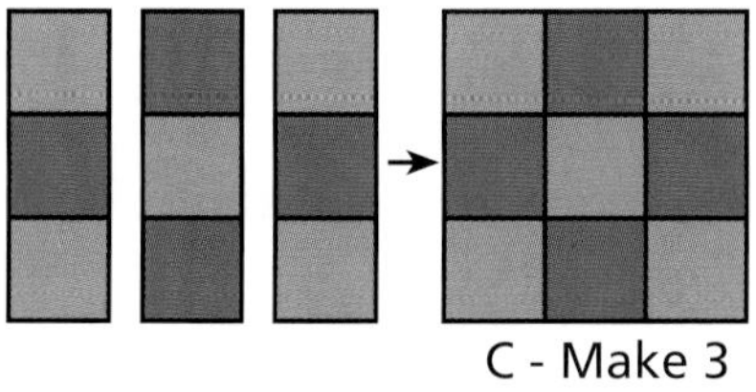

Diagram 5

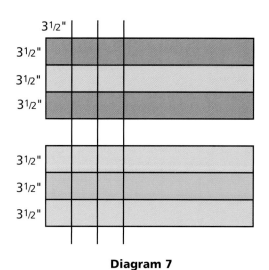

Diagram 7

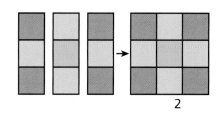

C - Make 3

Diagram 6

2

Diagram 8

5. Cut each Nine-Patch block into equal quarters. Measure 1½" from the seam line when cutting. (**Diagram 9**)

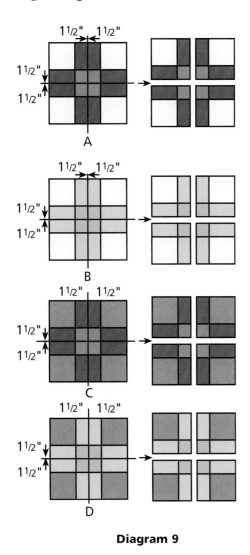

Diagram 9

6. Square the design units by trimming to 4¾" x 4¾".

7. Separate the quarter-units into four stacks by type, A, B, C, and D.

8. Pick up 16 quarter-units each from stacks A and B. Mark a diagonal pencil line from corner to corner on the wrong side of the unit. Mark from light corner to light corner. Repeat for all 32 units. This will be the sewing line. (**Diagram 10**)

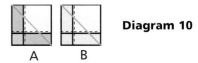

Diagram 10

9. Pick up two quarter-units each from stacks C and D. Mark a diagonal pencil line from corner to corner on the wrong side of the unit. Mark from light corner to light corner. Repeat for each of the four units. This will be the sewing line. (**Diagram 11**)

Diagram 11

10. Place a 4¾" red square right sides together with a quarter-unit. Sew the two squares together on the pencil line. Trim this unit ¼" from the stitching line. Repeat for all the quarter-units marked with pencil, **Diagram 12**. **Note:** *Be sure to trim along the correct side of stitching.*

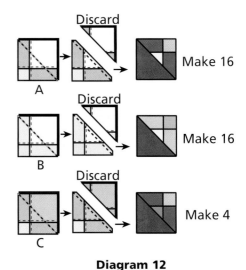

Diagram 12

110

11. Arrange the quarter-units to form a Tuscan Star block. Sew block together in rows and then sew rows together. (**Diagram 13**) Make four Tuscan Star blocks.

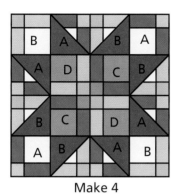

Make 4

Diagram 13

Quilt Assembly

1. Sew two Tuscan Star blocks together; repeat. Sew pairs together. (**Diagram 14**)

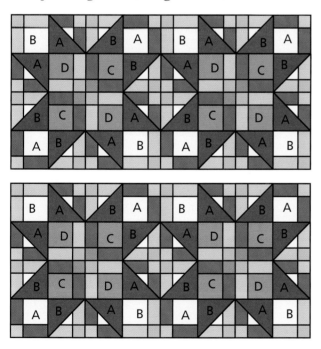

Diagram 14

Note: Refer to Borders with Corner Squares, page 17, to add border with corners.

2. Measure across the top and bottom of the quilt. Cut two 4³/4" light background strips to this measurement. Measure the sides of the quilt and cut two 4³/4" light background strips to this measurement.

3. Sew the border strips to the top and bottom of the quilt. Sew a quarter-unit to each end of the two remaining border strips. Sew to the sides of the quilt.

4. Layer top, batting and backing and quilt as desired.

5. Make 5 yards of straight grain binding. See General Directions, page 19, for making and applying binding.

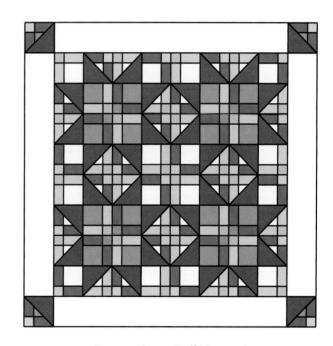

Tuscan Stars Quilt Layout

OTHER SIZES

	Baby/Small Lap	Twin	Double/Queen	King
Tucson Star Blocks 17" x 17"	6	15	20	36
Setting	2 x 3	3 x 5	4 x 5	6 x 6
9-Patch Starter Blocks	A - 9 B - 9 C - 4 D - 3	A - 23 B - 23 C - 9 D - 8	A - 30 B - 30 C - 11 D - 10	A - 54 B - 54 C - 19 D - 18
Size No Borders	34" x 51"	51" x 85"	68" x 85"	102" x 102"
Size with Border	42" x 59"	59" x 93"	76" x 93"	110" x 110"

Yardage

	Baby/Small Lap	Twin	Double/Queen	King
Background includes border	2 yards	3 yards	6½ yards	9½ yards
Blue	½ yard	¾ yard	1⅔ yards	2⅓ yards
Tan	½ yard	¾ yard	1⅔ yards	2⅓ yards
Gold	½ yard	¾ yard	1⅔ yards	2⅓ yards
Green	¼ yard	½ yard	⅔ yard	1½ yards
Red	1½ yards	2 yards	3½ yards	2½ yards
Binding Strips 2½" x width of fabric	5 yards	8 yards	9 yards	11 yards

Nautical Stars

The easy Star border is a fast way to set off the special nautical lighthouse novelty print. Construct these star blocks either by traditional Piece-by-Piece construction or Strip Sets. All fabrics are rotary cut.

Approximate Size: 33^1/$_2$" x 33^1/$_2$"
Four Starter Blocks: 9" finished
Block Size: 9" finished

MATERIALS

Note: Fabric quantities specified are for 42"/44"-wide, 100% cotton fabrics. All measurements include a ^{1}/$_4$-inch seam allowance unless otherwise specified in the instructions. Sew with right sides together unless otherwise stated. Press between each sewing step.

^{3}/$_4$ yard light blue fabric
^{1}/$_4$ yard medium blue fabric
^{1}/$_2$ yard white fabric
^{1}/$_2$ yard red fabric
^{1}/$_2$ yard novelty print
^{1}/$_3$ yard binding fabric
1^1/$_4$ yards backing fabric
1 yard batting

CUTTING

Blocks

4 muslin strips, 3^1/$_2$" x 22^1/$_2$"
1 muslin strip, 4" x width of fabric
2 light blue strips, 3^1/$_2$" x width of fabric
1 red strip, 4" x 22^1/$_2$"
1 medium blue strip, 4" x 22^1/$_2$"
32 light blue squares, 2" x 2"

Novelty Print Center

16^1/$_2$" x 16^1/$_2$"

Borders

2 medium blue strips, 1^1/$_2$" x 16^1/$_2$", first border
2 medium blue strips, 1^1/$_2$" x 18^1/$_2$", first border
4 light blue squares, 5" x 5", second (pieced) border
4 red strips, 3^3/$_4$" x width of fabric, third border

Binding

4 blue stripe strips, 2^1/$_2$" x width of fabric

INSTRUCTIONS

Design Units

Note: Refer to Strip-Set Panel Nine-Patch Construction, page 13, to make Nine-Patch blocks.

1. Sew 3^1/$_2$" light blue strip to each side of a 4" muslin strip. Cut at 3^1/$_2$" intervals. (**Diagram 1**)

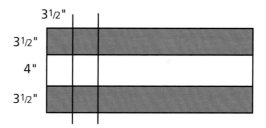

Diagram 1

2. Sew a 3½" x 22½" muslin strip to each side of a 4" medium blue strip. Cut at 4" intervals. Repeat with muslin and red strips. (**Diagram 2**)

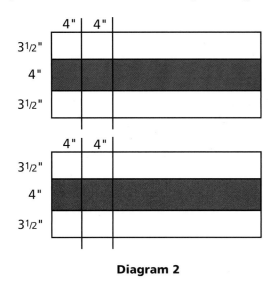

Diagram 2

3. Sew sub-units together to form Nine-Patch Starter blocks. (**Diagram 3**)

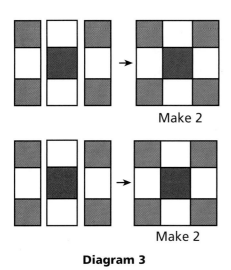

Make 2

Make 2

Diagram 3

4. Quarter-cut each Nine Patch block. Measure 1¾" from the inner seams for an accurate cut. (**Diagram 4**)

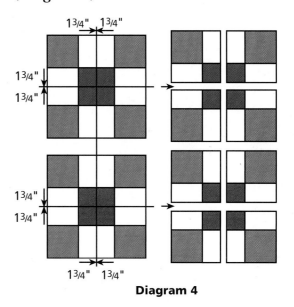

Diagram 4

5. Make a diagonal pencil line on each of the 32 light blue 2" x 2" squares. (**Diagram 5**)

   **Diagram 5**

6. Place a light blue square over the long rectangles of each quarter square. Sew along the pencil line. Trim away excess fabric under the small triangle and fold resulting triangle open to complete design units. (**Diagram 6**)

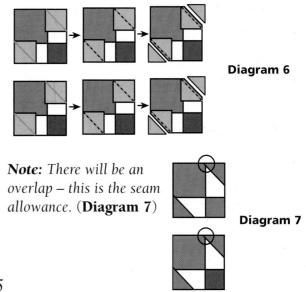

Diagram 6

Note: *There will be an overlap – this is the seam allowance.* (**Diagram 7**)

Diagram 7

115

Quilt Assembly

1. Sew 1½" x 16½" light blue strips to top and bottom of 16½" center square. Sew 1½" x 18½" light blue strips to sides. (**Diagram 8**)

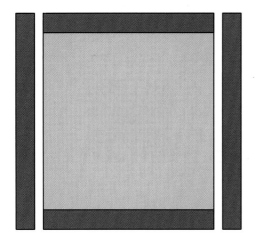

Diagram 8

2. For Star border, sew together four quarter-units. (**Diagram 9**) Repeat for three more strips.

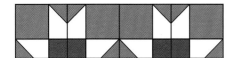

Diagram 9

3. Sew a pieced border strip to top and bottom of the quilt. Sew a 5" light blue square to each end of remaining border strips. Join to sides of quilt. (**Diagram 10**)

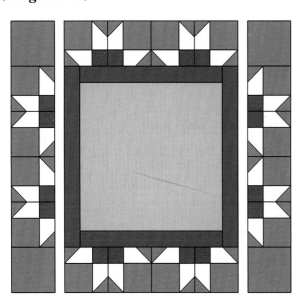

Diagram 10

4. Measure across top and bottom of quilt. Cut two 3¾" red strips to that measurement and sew to top and bottom of quilt. Measure length of quilt. Cut two 3¾" red strips to that length and sew to sides of quilt.

5. Layer backing, batting and quilt top. Quilt as desired.

6. Make 4 yards of straight grain binding. See General Directions, page 19, for making and applying binding.

Nautical Stars Quilt Layout

116

Plaid Stars

Instructions for this quilt are for traditional piece-by-piece construction. This technique is used to take advantage of assorted scraps in bright stripes and plaids. All fabrics are rotary cut. Pay close attention to the direction of the stripe fabrics during construction.

Approximate Size: 47¹/4" x 59¹/2"
Twelve Nine-Patch Starter Blocks: 12³/4" finished
Twelve Star Blocks: 12" finished

MATERIALS

Note: Fabric quantities specified are for 42"/44"-wide, 100% cotton fabrics. All measurements include a ¹/4-inch seam allowance unless otherwise specified in the instructions. Sew with right sides together unless otherwise stated. Press between each sewing step.

Blocks and Borders
¹/2 yard assorted plaid fabrics
¹/2 yard assorted stripe fabrics
2¹/2 yards black fabric
¹/3 yard bright green fabric
6 assorted bright scraps at least 5"-wide
6" square red

Binding
¹/2 yard black fabric

Backing and Batting
3¹/2 yards backing fabric
Twin-size batting

CUTTING

Nine-Patch Starter Blocks: 9" finished
24 plaid squares, 4³/4" x 4³/4"

24 stripe squares, 4³/4" x 4³/4"
54 black squares, 4³/4" x 4³/4"
96 black squares, 2³/8" x 2³/8"
6 assorted bright squares, 4³/4" x 4³/4"

Borders and Binding
5 green strips, 2¹/4" x width of fabric, first border
6 black strips, 4¹/2" x width of fabric, second border
6 strips, stripe fabric, 2¹/2" x width of fabric, binding

INSTRUCTIONS

Star Blocks
Note: Refer to Traditional Piece-byPiece Nine-Patch Construction, page 13, to make Nine-Patch blocks.

1. Sew 4³/4" black square to opposite sides of a 4³/4" stripe square noting position of stripes; repeat. Sew 4³/4" stripe square to 4³/4" bright square noting position of stripes. Sew rows together to form Nine-Patch A block. (**Diagram 1**) Make a total of six blocks.

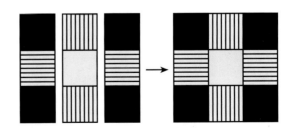

Diagram 1

117

2. Sew 4³/4" black square to opposite sides of a plaid square; repeat. Sew 4³/4" plaid square to opposite sides of 4³/4" black square. Sew rows together to complete Nine-Patch B block. (**Diagram 2**) Make a total of six blocks.

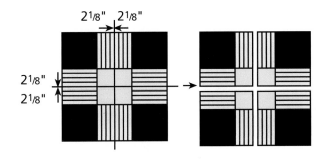

Diagram 2

3. Quarter-cut each Nine-Patch block. Measure 2¹/8" from the inside seam for an accurate cut. (**Diagram 3**)

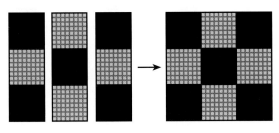

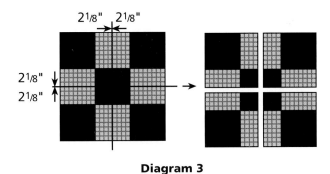

Diagram 3

4. Place a 2³/8" black square right sides together with stripe corner of quarter-unit; sew diagonally from corner to corner of black square. Repeat at opposite corner. (**Diagram 4**)

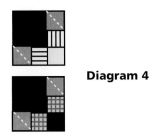

Diagram 4

5. Trim fabric ¹/4" from seam and flip resulting triangle over. (**Diagram 5**)

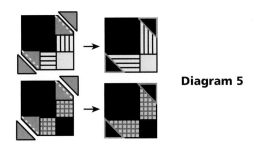

Diagram 5

Note: *There will be an overlap - this is the seam allowance.* (**Diagram 6**)

6. Trim quarter-units to 6¹/2" squares.

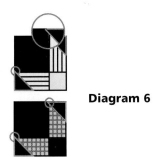

Diagram 6

7. Sort the quarter-units into plaid and stripe piles.

119

7. Lay out each block with two stripe quarter-units and two plaid quarter-units. Sew a plaid and stripe quarter-unit together; repeat. Sew pairs together to complete Star block. (**Diagram 7**) Make twelve Star blocks.

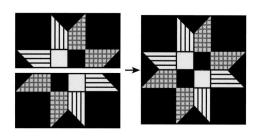

Diagram 7

8. Trim blocks to 12½" square.

Quilt Assembly

1. Lay out quilt in four horizontal rows of three blocks each. (**Diagram 8**)

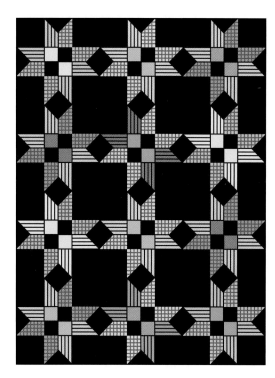

Diagram 8

2. Join the blocks in each row. Join the rows.

Note: *Refer to Adding Borders, page 16, to add borders.*

3. Measure quilt across top and bottom and cut two 2¼" green strips to that length. Measure length of quilt and cut two 2¼" green strips to that length.

4. Sew green border strips to top and bottom. Sew 2½" red square to each end of remaining border strips and sew to sides of quilt. (**Diagram 9**)

Diagram 9

120

5. Measure across top and bottom of quilt. Cut two 4¹/2" black strips to that length and sew to top and bottom of quilt. Measure length of quilt. Cut two 4¹/2" black strips to that length and attach to sides of quilt.

6. To use the quilting design included on page 122, trace pattern onto template plastic. Mark the quilting design as desired, adjusting it to fit your quilt.

Tip: The template is slightly undersized to allow for individual sewing habits and seam allowances. Center and mark the template, then stretch the design as you stitch with additional stitches between each marked design. Make a note of how this is done at the corners on the black border.

7. Layer top, batting and backing and quilt as desired.

8. Make 7 yards of straight grain binding. See General Directions, page 19, for making and applying binding.

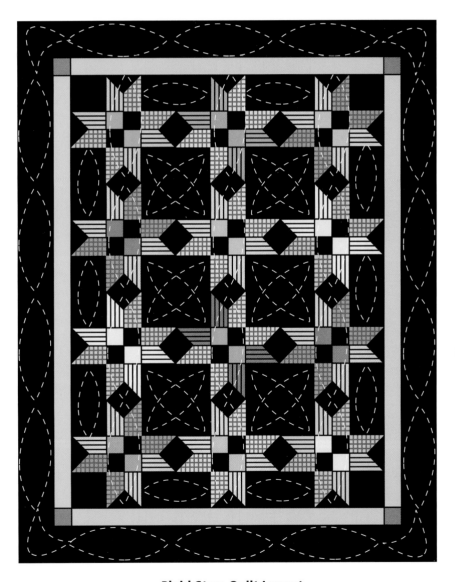

Plaid Stars Quilt Layout

121

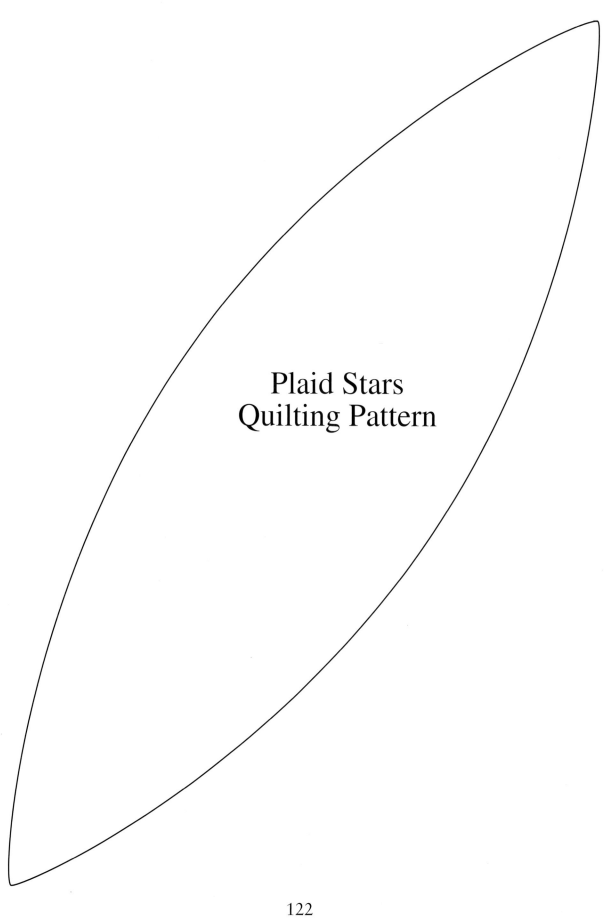

Plaid Stars
Quilting Pattern

OTHER SIZES

	Twin	Double/Queen	King
Nine Patch Blocks	35 blocks	56 blocks	64 blocks
Blocks Set	5 x 7	7 x 8	8 x 8
Size (no borders)	61 1/4" x 85 3/4"	85 3/4" x 98"	98" x 98"
First Border Strips with Corner Squares	8 @ 2 1/4" x width with 4 corner squares Adds 3 1/2"	10 @ 2 1/4" x width with 4 corner squares Adds 3 1/2"	11 @ 2 1/4" x width with 4 corner squares Adds 3 1/2"
Second Border Strips	8 @ 4 1/2" x width Adds 8"	10 @ 4 1/2" x width Adds 8"	11 @ 4 1/2" x width Adds 8"
Binding Strips	9 @ 2 1/2" x width	10 @ 2 1/2" x width	12 @ 2 1/2" x width
Finished Size	71 1/2" x 95 1/2"	95 1/2" x 107 1/2"	107 1/2" x107 1/2"

Yardage

	Twin	Double/Queen	King
Assorted Plaids	1 1/2 yards	2 1/2 yards	2 3/4 yards
Assorted Strips	1 1/2 yards	2 1/2 yards	2 3/4 yards
Bright Squares	18 squares, 4 3/4"	29 squares, 4 3/4"	33 squares, 4 3/4"
Black	4 yards	4 3/4 yards	6 1/2 yards
First Border	5/8 yard	3/4 yard	7/8 yard
Second Border and Binding	1 3/4 yards	2 yards	2 1/4 yards

Provincial Stars

Construct these star blocks either by traditional Piece-by-Piece construction or Strip Sets. The sample quilt takes advantage of assorted scraps in bright Provincial fabrics. All fabrics are rotary cut.

Approximate Size: 55" x 67"
Twelve Starter Nine-Patch Blocks:
9" finished
Block Size: 9 1/2" finished

MATERIALS

Notes: Fabric quantities specified are for 42"/44"-wide, 100% cotton fabrics. All measurements include a 1/4-inch seam allowance unless otherwise specified in the instructions. Sew with right sides together unless otherwise stated. Press between each sewing step.

To make a scrap quilt use equivalent yardage in assorted scrap fabrics.

Provincial Star Blocks, Borders and Binding
2 1/4 yards muslin
2 yards print fabric
1 7/8 yards yellow print

Backing and Batting
4 yards backing fabric
Twin-size batting

CUTTING

Blocks
4 strips muslin, 3 1/2" x width of fabric
2 strips print fabric, 4" x width of fabric
2 strips print fabric, 3 1/2" x width of fabric
4 strips muslin, 2" x width of fabric, cut into 96 squares

Sashing Bars and Small Nine-Patch Blocks
18 print fabric strips, 1 1/2" x width of fabric
11 muslin strips, 1 1/2" x width of fabric

Borders
8 muslin strips, 3 1/2" x width of fabric
8 yellow print strips, 5 1/2" x width of fabric

Binding
8 yellow print strips, 2 1/2" x width of fabric

INSTRUCTIONS

Provincial Star Blocks
Note: Refer to Strip-Set Panel Nine-Patch Construction, page 13, to make Starter Nine-Patch blocks.

1. Sew a 3 1/2" muslin strip to each side of a 4" print strip; cut at 3 1/2" intervals. (**Diagram 1**)

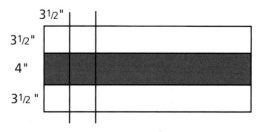

Diagram 1

2. Sew a 3½" print strip to each side of a 4" print strip; cut at 4" intervals. (**Diagram 2**)

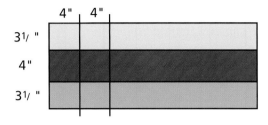

Diagram 2

3. Sew sub-units together to form Nine-Patch block. (**Diagram 3**) Make twelve Nine-Patch blocks.

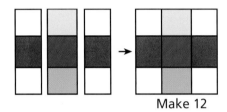

Make 12

Diagram 3

4. Quarter cut each Nine-Patch block. Measure 1¾" from the seam line for an accurate cut. (**Diagram 4**) Arrange in groups of four.

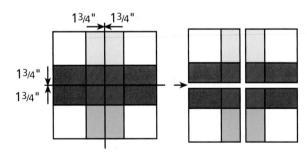

Diagram 4

5. Make a diagonal pencil line on wrong side of each of the 2" muslin squares.

6. Place a marked muslin square over the long rectangles of a quarter-unit; sew along the drawn pencil line. (**Diagram 5**)

Diagram 5

7. Trim away excess fabric under the small triangle. (**Diagram 6**)

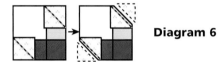

Diagram 6

Note: *There will be an overlap – this is the seam allowance.* (**Diagram 7**)

Diagram 7

8. Lay out four quarter-units for each Provincial Star block; sew units together in pairs and then sew pairs together. (**Diagram 8**)

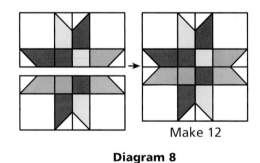

Make 12

Diagram 8

9. Square, by trimming the blocks to 9½".

Quilt Assembly

1. For strip set A, sew a 1½" print strip to each side of a 1½" muslin strip. (**Diagram 9**)

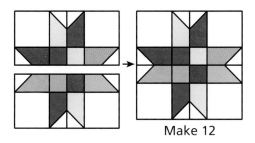

Make 12

Diagram 9

Note: Use two different print strips. Make nine strip sets.

2. Cut strip set at 9½" intervals for sashing strips. (**Diagram 10**) Make 31 sashing strips. Reserve the scraps for the small Nine-Patch cornerstones.

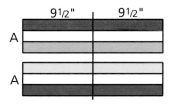

Diagram 10

3. For strip set B, sew a 1½" muslin strip to each side of a 1½" print strip. (**Diagram 11**)

Diagram 11

4. Cut strip sets A and B at 1½" intervals. (**Diagram 12**) Sew sub-units together to make small Nine-Patch cornerstones. (**Diagram 13**) Make 24 small Nine-Patch blocks.

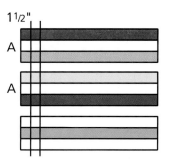

Diagram 12

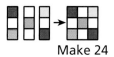

Make 24

Diagram 13

5. Sew three quilt sashing bars alternating with four small Nine-Patch cornerstones. (**Diagram 14**) Make five sashing rows.

Make five sashing rows

Diagram 14

6. Sew four sashing bars alternating with three Provincial Star blocks. (**Diagram 15**) Make four block rows

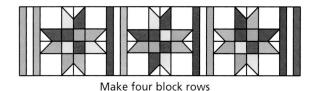

Make four block rows

Diagram 15

7. Sew the sashing and block rows together. (**Diagram 16**)

Diagram 16

Note: Refer to Adding the Borders, page 16, to add borders.

8. Measure across the top and bottom of the quilt and cut two 3½" muslin strips to this measurement. Measure the quilt lengthwise and cut two 3½" muslin strips to this measurement.

9. Sew border strips to the top and bottom of the quilt. Sew a small Nine-Patch cornerstone to each end of remaining 3½" muslin strips and sew to sides of quilt.

10. Measure across top and bottom of quilt. Cut two 5½" yellow strips to this measurement and sew to top and bottom of quilt. Measure quilt lengthwise. Cut two 5½" yellow strips to this measurement and sew to sides of quilt.

11. Layer backing, batting and quilt top and quilt as desired.

12. Make 6½ yards of straight grain binding. See General Directions, page 19, for making and applying binding.

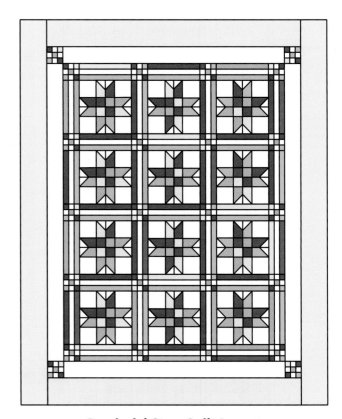

Provincial Stars Quilt Layout